WICCA FO]

Wicca Starter Kit: Book to Learn the Secrets of Witchcraft with Wiccan Spells, Moon Rituals, and Tools Like Tarots, Meditation, Herbal Power, Crystal magic and candle

Astrology and Numerology Academy

TABLE OF CONTENTS

Introduction..4

Chapter 1 Overview of Wicca 6

Chapter 2 The Benefits of Wicca........................ 20

Chapter 3: Step by Step Guide to Rituals 23

    Your Tool Kit 23

    Stones and Crystals 29

    Setting Up Your Altar 30

    Asking the Gods/Goddesses for Support.............. 33

    Casting Your Circle 35

    Spells, Rituals, Intentions 39

    Closing Your Circle... 43

    Accepting Your True Power.............................. 45

Chapter 4: Love and Relationship Spells 47

    Spell for New Friendships 47

    Charm for Attracting Quality Relationships............ 48

    Romance Attraction Smudge 50

    Stellar First Date Confidence Charm............... 52

    Ritual Bath for a Blind Date............................ 53

    Relationship Potential Divine "Forecast" 55

    Choosing Peace in Tough Situations................ 58

    "Spare Key" Spell for Spiritual Connection 60

Chapter 5 : Herbal Magic: Rituals and Spells 64

Chapter 6: Spells for Wealth 84

    Herbs of Prosperity 84

Bowl of Change.. 84

Mandrake Money 85

Abundance Candle Spell 85

The Self-Love Spell... 85

Invitation of Love Spell.. 87

Fire Flowers Spell 90

Wealth Attraction Bath 92

Law of Abundance Spell.. 93

Lavender Money Spell 93

Mint Prosperity Spell 94

Chapter 7: The basic and advance practice of candle
magic.. 95

Types of Candles 95

Colors and What They Mean to a Wiccan 98

The Intent behind the Days of the Week..................... 101

Candle Magic Spell for Drawing Money.................... 103

Candle Magic Spell to Celebrate Imbolc 106

Chapter 8: Casting Circles... 111

Simple Circle Cast 114

Advanced Circle Casting... 116

Circle Casting... 117

Chapter 9: Meditation and Dreams 120

How to Do a Wiccan Meditation................................. 135

Conclusion 139

Introduction

Welcome to the wide world of Wicca, a set of beliefs, rituals, and traditions that has swept across the Western world since the mid-twentieth century. Immerse yourself in a system of belief that connects us back to nature and to the spiritual realm, all while undertaking self-care and personal empowerment. We are all interconnected—with each other, with the earth and the physical realm, with the spiritual energy that flows throughout the universe. Take advantage of such knowledge to build a life of intention and fulfillment.

In order to begin understanding what Wicca is and what the religion can mean to you, it is also important to understand just what Wicca is not. The reason this is important is that there is a lot of misinformation that exists in the world about Wicca. In an attempt to preserve your relationship to nature as you go through the journey into Wicca, it is crucial that you separate the white noise from the truth of Wicca.

Wicca is not a cult. This is a critical point that you need to understand if you are going to have a relationship with the world as a Wiccan. Also, the practice of witchcraft does not mean you have joined a cult either.

Essentially, to become Wiccan means to hold all life in high regard. Since Wiccans can and do practice spell magic, this is what this book will essentially be about. The main goal of this book is to introduce you to beginner's spells and magic that you can use in your

4

everyday life as a Wiccan witch. There are spells that are meant to be performed by covens, but for the purposes of this guide, I will not include them.

I will focus on the magic that you can accomplish as an individual. If you are still trying to find your way in the Wicca religion and are still practicing your hand at spells, then this book is definitely what you have been looking for.

To be Wiccan does not necessitate that you have to be a part of a coven. There are quite a few Wiccans that practice their religion and magic on their own. This is what this guide focuses on—your personal journey into the world of Wicca and witchcraft.

Wicca is an amazing journey that heightens your relationship with the world but, like with any religion, it is founded on some basic principles and rules.

Wicca is, at its very core, an inclusive belief system that emphasizes our relationships with the natural and spiritual realms. Anyone who wishes to channel their energy into a positive and powerful life of intention and achievement can begin by practicing Wicca today!

Chapter 1 Overview of Wicca

Wicca is a way of life, often called a religion. It lays the groundwork for people to live and work harmoniously with the world around them. When you live life the Wiccan way, you are living in a way that encourages togetherness with the godly and with everything that has been brought into existence from the Divine.

When you choose to live life the Wiccan way, you agree to live in profound awe and appreciation of the world around you. You are expressing gratitude for the world that you experience from the sunrise and sunset to the growing and harvesting of plants and the natural lifecycles of the animals around you. Everything that is a part of your natural world becomes sacred to you as you see it as being a sacred gift afforded to you by the world surrounding you.

This particular belief system predates Christianity, and it originates in Ireland, Scotland and Wales. There, the ancient ancestors learned how to live together in unity with the world around them, honoring the Divine in everything and cherishing all that was. Much of the information that is used in modern Wicca stems from these ancient traditions, although there is plenty of modern information and twists that have been incorporated into the tradition since.

It is important to understand that Wicca has multiple "types" of belief systems to it. Plenty of off-shoots of the original traditions have developed, allowing for many different types of belief systems to be incorporated into their lifestyle. This way, regardless of what your beliefs are, you will likely find someone in the Wiccan faith who believes similarly to you, allowing you to connect with others who can help you advance your own practices and learn more about yourself and this intricate belief system.

We are but a part of the Earth, no greater and no less than any other creature that crawls, flies, or swims. Thus, it is our duty to care for, heal, and protect every being that exists. To be Wiccan is to give selflessly, to take on the role of a teacher, and to go on a continuous quest for improvement.

To be Wiccan is to recognize power in everything and every creature that you behold. As Wiccan, it is for you to see the divine power in whatever face it chooses to manifest itself. That face can be in the form of the naked tree branches shivering in the autumn wind or in the promise held by each petal of a budding flower in spring.

The medieval church made great efforts to demonize the image of the Wiccan faith. But if anything else, to be Wiccan means to become a promoter of peace and to lead by example by living a violence-free lifestyle. Our goal is to co-exist in harmony with all creatures in this Earth and with the divine powers that surround us.

As Wiccan, it is important for you to understand that we do not acknowledge the idea of an absolute evil such as

Satan. Unlike believers of other religions, Wiccans are not driven by fear of "punishment in the afterlife" or "eternal damnation." Instead, Wiccans are encouraged to be kind to others and to "behave" in this life simply because it is the right thing to do.

Another misconception that is as old as time is the idea of Wicca as a cult. Increasing our numbers and manipulating people's heads to gain power has never been the Wiccan way. On the contrary, to be Wiccan is all about embracing diversity. As Wiccans, we always respect and uphold the individual's right to choose the way he wants to live his life.

Does this mean that there are no rules that govern the Wiccan faith?

As a religion, Wicca functions with a basic set of rules. The first among these set of principles is the Wiccan Rede which states that as long as you harm none, you are free to do as you choose. It is because of this rule that Wiccans are discouraged to use magick to intentionally harm another living being.

To be Wiccan means to be in sync with the universe. Thus, you will be able to tap into the infinite pool of universal wisdom and gain access to the knowledge of magick. That privilege is accompanied by a great responsibility. As Wiccan, you are encouraged to use magick exclusively for doing good.

According to the Law of Threefold Return, whatever energy you send out into the world, whether it's negative or positive, will return to you and when it does, it shall be three times stronger. It is important to note that this rule is by no means a way to reassure obedience by striking fear. The universe does not seek to punish anyone. This is simply a natural reaction. Think of the universe as a vast ocean of energy which connects and encompasses the individual energies of all living beings, including you.

When you send out ripples of energy, be it in the form of an action or an intention, it will be released into that vast ocean and will touch everything and everyone. But just like ocean waves, that energy will eventually return to touch you as well.

In the '70's, there was a rise in horrible criminal activities done by members of satanic cults. Sadly, the media wrongly associated these activities with Wiccans and these misconceptions were spread among the public. Feeling the threat, the Council of Witches formed the 13 Principles of Wiccan Belief to regulate Wiccan practice.

Up until today, a great number of covens use this model when creating mandates. The main idea behind these principles is that we are to care for nature just as we must allow nature to care for us. Within us lies an innate power which we must control and wield so that we are able to live in harmony with nature and with all beings.

Each of us consists of internal and external dimensions, inner and outer realities, and it is our duty to nurture both dimensions. As Wiccan, you must appreciate the universe's creative power which is revealed through the merging of the masculine and the feminine energies. To Wiccans, sex is symbolic of life and a source of energy which can be powerful when used in magick.

Additionally, it is necessary to note that different covens are run by different rules created by their committees. Such rules serve to guide you in the prudent use of magick. Each coven is ruled by the High Priestess or the High Priest. To become a member of a coven is to agree to live according to these rules.

You also have the option to become a solitary practitioner. Whichever path you choose, remember that the goodness in your heart, your conscience, and the purity of your intention is a far greater guide than any rule set in stone.

What is Magick?

Belief in magick is an essential part of the Wiccan religion. In the simplest sense, magick means harnessing the energy of the universe to make something happen. Everything in this universe is made up of energy. You are made up of energy. And all of our energies are interconnected by what is called the Universal Energy that flows freely and endlessly around us. Everyone was born with the ability to tap into and wield these energies to create a certain effect.

As Wiccan, you must believe that it is your birthright to access this illimitable supply of energy so that you may improve your life and those of others. Tapping into this energy and using it is done through magick and spellcasting. Each time you cast a spell; you are borrowing energy from the divine essence of the universe. You can understand now why spellcasting should be a sacred act and is not to be taken lightly. It is not for you to abuse the powers of the universe. Practicing Wiccans utilize magick for meaningful endeavors such as to help a friend recover from an illness or from grief, to attract love for others of for oneself, to heal the Earth, or to invite happiness into one's life.

Wicca Core Beliefs and Philosophies

Wicca can be described as a broad religion as it has the happiness of including a lot of different perspectives, realities and beliefs. There are, however, several major core beliefs that are practiced by a majority of Wiccans as a way to establish a grounding basis for understanding the magic you are working with when you are practicing.

These concepts are taken into account, no matter what coven you are in, or what deity you are worshipping. The concepts outlined in this chapter are main platform, or foundation, of what Wicca is and how it explains itself to anyone wishing to follow this path.

Nature is Divine

A majority of Wiccans will tell you that nature is divine. It is like a backbone to the entire practice and there are so many ways that this core belief manifests itself in these rituals. We are all members of this Earth: every rock, tree, leaf, plant, animal, bird, insect, and person, not to mention hundreds of thousands of other species and landscapes.

The Earth is or sacred home and we are a sacred part of it. It is where all life energy is stored and recreated and we are a part of those cycles and systems. To worship nature is to worship the very essence of all things. And you will find that all Wiccan holidays and festivals that are celebrated are derived from a worship of nature. Each festival is marked by a solstice or equinox. All esbats are marked by the cycle of the moon. And just about every ingredient in the rituals and spells of these festivities comes from nature somehow.

There is also a celebration in nature of the unity of opposing forces. There is always a balance of the light and the dark and nature-worship provides the opportunity to look at life from that place of balance and serenity. It is the presence of the male and female in all things; the yin and the yang. That is nature.

The practice of devoting space and love to nature is a part of the Wiccan creed and even though it is not a demand that you follow that practice, it comes naturally when you consider all of the other core beliefs.

Many of the tools that you will use for your rituals and spells are derived from nature. You will find yourself gathering herbs or pieces of wood for making a wand. You may be harvesting certain plants to hang around your house for a certain holiday, or dressing your altar in the perfumes and trinkets of the forest floor. All of nature comes into Wicca and it is a powerful process to fully connect with the divine in nature.

Karma, The Afterlife and Reincarnation

Karma is an echo of what you may find in the Threefold Law (see below) which basically states that what you do in this life carries over into your next one. To make such a suggestion, one must believe in the concept of reincarnation, which creates an open doorway for your spiritual being and essence to return to another life, after your last one, to continue to learn lessons and acquire knowledge for the evolution of all things.

According to Wicca, this is what will always be and has always been, and so in order to adopt the principles of Wicca, you must look into the reality of who you were before, and who you are going to be next. It might be that you are already familiar with some of your past life experiences and you already know what lessons you are trying to learn from those lives. In other cases, for some, you gain new knowledge as you go and are not always privy to what you are supposed to be learning. The concept of Karma asks that you remind yourself what you need to heal from your former lives so that you can ascend further into your true power and magic. And while you are at it, in this life you are living now, be sure that what you do is something you want to take with you into the next life.

Although there is the concept of reincarnation, there is also the concept of the afterlife, sometimes referred to as Summerland, and it is here that you rest between lives to prepare for the next one, to gather your strength and reflect on the journey before to create the best journey forward.

All of these concepts help the Wiccan to bridge the gap between Earth and Spirit and that the balance of the divine is always present, no matter what life you are living, or what stage of travel you are in between worlds.

Ancestors

It is not uncommon to call upon the ancestors in the practice of Wiccan rituals and casting. Many Wiccans believe that our ancestors are always with us, guiding us and showing us the way and should be honored for their own commitment to forging ahead and living life.

Wiccans celebrate deities of various kinds and it is normal to include your ancestors in your practice just as frequently, as they are a part of the cycle of the self and have many lessons to teach as you grow and honor your own path. The concept of honoring the ancestors in not specific to Wicca and is a cross-cultural truth, present in most religious practices.

A great deal of worship for the ancestors comes from a need to embrace the past as well as what your ancestors continue to do for you in the future.

Wheel of the Year

All of the cycles of the year are celebrated in Wicca. Every solstice has a celebration, or Sabbat, and every equinox, too. The rituals and spells that accompany these times are a sacred honoring and celebration committed to the end of something to hail the beginning of something new. In the calendar of the year, there are endless deaths and rebirths that can occur and as a Wiccan, you will find harmony and abundance with every passing season because of that very truth: life begets death which begets more life.

In all of the seasons there are also moon cycles that are celebrated throughout the ritual of Esbats. The cycles of the moon organize the seasons and every waning moon leads to an ending, into a darkening, while every waxing moon leads to a powerful fullness that has its own magic and ritual associated with it.

All of the rhythms and cycles are a part of Wiccan work and it will be a part of this world forever. The concept of worshiping the divine in nature goes closely with the wheel of the year and should be counted as a major component of Wiccan worship.

Personal Responsibility and Responsibility

This concept agrees with the Wiccan Rede and the Threefold Law. You are responsible for every action you take. Wicca asks that you are wise to your power because it might be more than you realize, especially when you are working with the sacred divine energies of all things and all life.

When you are practicing Wicca, you are becoming responsible for more than just yourself; you are using the energy of all life to celebrate and support the life you lead and everything you choose can have an impact on another. It is a wonderful way for you to be honest with the truth of karma as well, because whatever you are responsible for in this life, goes with you forward into the next.

You are incredibly powerful, and Wicca helps you to embrace your internal power and life force energy; it also asks you to be responsible with your power and to harm none and do right by your actions and rituals.

The Wiccan Rede: Harm None

The Wiccan Rede simply states that you should do nothing in your practice that could cause harm to another individual. The basic concept of the golden rule of thumb, that you would do unto others, but it is also asking you to be very cautious in your practice and to consider how you are wording your spells and rituals.

The practice of Wicca is meant to be of benefit to the greater good of all life and so a lot of it has to do with intentions. When you are practicing you might find that you need to state that you are wanting to harm none and that you will uphold the good of all living things on Earth, so it be in your power.

You will find this credo in all of the Wiccan books you find and it has held steady and true for some time. It holds you to your personal responsibility and power and that you have to be the one to make the right choice when using the gift of magic.

Equality

Coercion is not an element of the Wiccan faith. Proselytizing is frowned upon and an aura of acceptance for all backgrounds and spiritual purposes is embraced. Wiccans generally believe that there needs to be an equality in all matters and that all people have a right to walk their own spiritual path; the one that is right for them.

The concept of equality should go without saying in all religions, but unfortunately this is often not the case. This is one way that Wicca is so unique; it offers a way to receive wisdom and abundance through worship of the divine without suggesting that it can only be done a certain way.

Wicca equals equality and the practicing of this artful religion requires an open heart and an open mind to anyone who is in need of a spiritual community and path.

Rule of Three

The Threefold Law, aka Rule of Three, is used in many Wiccan traditions. Not everyone supports this law, however it comes up often and should be noted, or practiced if it suits you. This concept states that whatever spell or magical act is being performed, the resulting energy created from that act will go into the Universe, and come back to the practitioner three times.

You may or may not be familiar with this concept, and it has origins in other cultural practices, especially those of Eastern religions that believe in the law of karma. Wicca is what gives it the concept of three times, the number bearing importance to the reality of the power you are wielding.

It might not happen in the way that you think, for example if you wish harm on someone else, you may have three separate instances of bad fortune as a result, or it could feel like the impact of the return is 3 times greater than it normally would be, like expecting to get paid $100 and getting paid $300.

The Threefold Law is just another way to help you keep a balance with your practice and ensure that you harm none, and that includes harming yourself with the energy of three coming back to you.

Elements in All Things

In Wiccan belief, there are five elements: earth, air, fire, water, ether, or spirit. During rituals and ceremonies and especially in the casting or consecrating of a circle, the five elements are called into balance the energies of the ritual or spell. Not all Wiccans practice with five elements and just use the 4 main ones, conserving spirit as represented by the deity that they worship.

These elements are the fundamental building blocks of all things on Earth and in the Universe. They are responsible for the great eternal cycle of life through creation and destruction, the birth-death-rebirth cycle. These forces of nature that are sacred to Wiccans are always a part of practice because they are the literal life force that binds all matter and all spirit.

These elements have been studied throughout time and were part of philosophies dating back to the early Greeks, who were also worshippers of deities and religions of nature. These concepts are found across continents throughout many religions and beliefs including in Egypt and Babylonia, Hinduism and Buddhism, and many more.

The elements are definitely a tool that must be used in your Wiccan practice and as you get further along in your understanding of your spell work and rituals, you will find how important and powerful they can truly be.

Chapter 2 The Benefits of Wicca

Wicca has many aspects as a spiritual practice. There's no way to practice magic, and there's no way to practice magic. People practice magic from all sects, cultures, and for a variety of reasons. That being said, there are a variety of fundamental characteristics that can help those who work. Here are the twelve advantages of wick:

Anyone Can Be A Wicca – Wicca is often associated with the Wicca faith, but one doesn't have to be Wiccan to practice Wicca. Those from all religious backgrounds practice sorcery, and so do non-religious people.

There Are No Rules – Yes, there are spell books, manuals, resources, and a variety of things that people recommend, but the ritual is yours, and it can be as complicated or as simple as you like.

You Can Do It From Anywhere – A lot of Wiccans have named holy places and altars to practice spells, but in fact, they can be practiced anywhere. All you need is you, your goal, and a place where you can concentrate.

Time In Nature – One of the most significant benefits of Wicca is that it helps you spend more time outdoors, interacting with nature, meditating, and having a more significant appreciation for your environment. It also gives you time to unplug the phone.

Knowledge – Wicca requires a lot of training, and you never really stop learning. You will learn a lot about plants and their medicinal properties, the phases of the moon, nature, flowers, trees, animals, crystals, yoga, chakras, natural healing, tea, mythology, history, and the magic of all these things. You should know more about yourself, too!

Knowing What You Want – Spellwork needs you to be explicit about your goal, and that can give you a lot of insight into what you want in life. As a consequence, it can help you take more action to move towards these issues.

Time To De-Stress – Wicca is, at its core, a spiritual practice focused on nature. As Earth's children, few things can make our minds easier than connecting with nature and the elements. It also lets you meditate and think regularly.

There Are Many Paths – Since there is no way to practice magic, you should find the path that most people identify with. You could be a green wick, a sea wick, or a hedge wick. You should meet in a coven or on your own. You can obey the spell books or create rituals of your own.

Reasons To Celebrate – There are many holy days in which some Wiccan celebrate, including the summer and winter solstices, the spring and autumn equinoxes, Samhain, Beltane, and others. People celebrate in different ways, but they often involve cooking a special feast, ceremonies, nature walks, reflection, remembering ancestors, bonfires, and appreciation.

Inspiration – A lot of wicks share their inspiration, positivity, and joy with others, and social media make it easy to consume all that wisdom.

It's Inclusive – One reason I think that Wiccan resonates with so many people is that it's welcoming. This empowers women and does not discriminate against LGBT people. This gives people space to explore faith in a judgment-free environment that also encourages compassion, self-care, harmony, and healing.

It Promotes Healthy Habits – Drinking tea, cooking with herbs, spending time outside, reading and dreaming, meditation, being honest about what you want, communicating with the environment, taking care of the earth, taking care of animals, reading books, and sharing your feelings are all things that you can do more if you practice Wicca.

Chapter 3: Step by Step Guide to Rituals

Practicing magik is easy. All you need is a few tools, a place to set up an altar, and clear intentions. The following step-by-step guide will help you on your path to opening yourself up to the most basic form of rituals, spells and meditations. You don't have to follow these rules in order to cast; you can use them as a foundation to work from and get ideas to create your own powerful rituals and spells.

A lot of Wicca is intuition and connection to your higher self and your own divine wisdom and authority. Let yourself be a guide as you determine the best ways to invoke the right power, energy and intention to bring more abundance and prosperity into your life.

As you get started, look around your house for some of these tools. You don't have to rush out to the store and buy a bunch of new items to make your altar or prepare your spells. So much of what you will use you can find around your house until something better, or more intentional, comes along.

Your Tool Kit

A witch's basic tool kit requires only a few things which you can find in the list below. There are other items that you can consider optional while you are getting started until you are able to build up your tool chest of magical properties and elements.

- Candle(s)/ candle holder

- Matches/ lighter

- Salt

- Stones/ crystals (optional)

- Incense/ or smudge stick (preferably sage)

- Dish of clean water in a glass, or wooden bowl (not plastic)

These very basic tools are all you really need to get started. As you play around more and advance, you can add things that bear meaning to your ritual or spell that you are casting. Some Wiccans like to keep figures of their preferred deities to have present, or to place on the altar you create. You can also bring more herbs into the ritual as you see fit, but ultimately, all you need to start with are the items on the list above.

You don't need an altar to use these tools. You can even carry them with you to places out in nature or wherever you are casting magik and can consider it your traveling toolbox for making magik.

The candle brings fire to your ceremony, one of the elements that you will need to call into your circle. The matches and the lighter are to light both the candle(s) and the incense. Salt is a powerful protective agent. Some people cast their circles by making a salt circle around their bodies and their tools, but you can also just keep it with you in a box or a tin to have it as a representation of the Earth energy and also as a symbol of protection.

The stones and crystals, although optional, can come in handy and are very helpful for magnifying and intensifying energy; so whatever ritual or spell you are performing, your chosen stones/crystals can help enhance that experience and bring more energy to it. All stones and crystals have their own unique properties and so finding the ones that resonate most with you will be a significant part of your journey.

The incense/ smudge stick is used to purify the energy around you and cleanse the aura of the room and your own auras. You can use it before, during, and after your ritual to help you feel balanced and attuned to your spells.

Candles

Candles play a major part in any ritual. We have all used the light of candles since we learned how to create our own lasting light and the candle is a great symbol of life in the practice of Wicca.

The act of lighting a candle is a powerful energetic vibration of intention and opens a doorway for you to connect more deeply with the powerful magik you are wanting to invoke. Using candles in all of your ritual and spell work is a good way to bring that energy and focus forward.

Sometimes, you may want to have a candle in a container so that you can burn it overnight or until it burns out. Letting the sacred flame of your spell work continue to burn is a way of energetically stating that your intentions will stay alive until the next candle is lit.

You will also want to find candles that might correlate with your spells based on their colors. Here is a list of what each candle color might represent in a spell you are working:

White – Purity, unity, peace, cleansing, innocence, balance, healing, magik involving young children, spirituality, aura balancing

Yellow – Success, happiness, joy, pleasure, concentration, learning, solar/sun magik, confidence, travel, memory, imagination, flexibility, air element

Orange – Opportunity, creativity, joy, investments, legal matters, justice, self-expression, overcoming addictions, success in business, ambition, vitality, fun

Pink – Feminine energy, compassion, love, romance, domestic bliss, partnerships, friendships, protection of children, nurturing, self-improvement

Red – Vitality, passion, courage, sexual potency, fertility, survival, fire element, independence, conflict, competition, war, danger

Purple – Contact with spirits, independence, wisdom, influence, breaking habits, changing luck, banishing evil energy or dark forces, spiritual power

Blue – Focus, forgiveness, communication, truth, fidelity, good fortune, astral projection, water element, sincerity, patience, domestic harmony, lifting bad/low vibrations

Green – Physical and emotional healing, luck, growth, acceptance, marriage, prosperity, abundance, dispel/counteract jealousy or greed, tree and plant magik

Brown – Earth magik and earth element, stability, material goods or wealth, construction, real estate/ house magik, house blessings, animal, and pet magik

Black – Protection, safety, repelling black magik, reversing hexes, defense, banishing negative vibrations, grounding, wisdom, scrying, pride

Silver – Psychic awareness, lucid dreams and dream states, meditation, communication, feminine energies, victory, stability, moon magik, luck with gambling

Gold – Masculine energies, prosperity, abundance, sun/solar energy, positive vibrations, divination, great fortune, attraction, luxury, health, justice

You don't have to use colorful candles to cast spells or practice rituals. Any kind of candle will work and you can use them in whatever way feels safest and best. Using the colored candles will offer an extra boost of energy and intention to your spell and craft work. Color magik and candle magik are both very potent and powerful energies and when combined together they make for a great force of light and alignment with your intentions in your practice.

Smudging

Smudging is an ancient ceremonial practice and involves the burning of sacred herbs that create a pungent and aromatic smoke that cleanses and purifies. Using a smudge stick, or bundle of dried herbs, in your ceremonies is of great benefit and should be practiced as often as you like.

When you use a smudge stick in your spells and rituals, you are energetically purifying the space around you and protecting your energy from unwanted energies that may be drawn to you. You can use the smoke of your smudge stick to draw a wide circle around the space you will be casting in. You can also use salt in the same way but often the mess is harder to clean up, unless you are outside.

Smudging is a beautiful ceremonial tool and you can do it before, during, and after your incantations and rituals. Some of the most popular smudge sticks are:

- Sage

- Cedar

- Sweet grass

- Lavender

- Juniper

- Mugwort

- Palo Santo (sacred wood, not herbs)

Any of these would work in your ceremonies and craft works. You can even make your own. All you need is the herb of your choice. Tie it in a bundle with string while it is freshly cut. Hang it to dry upside down. Use when needed.

Stones and Crystals

Stones and crystals, each have unique qualities and characteristics. Some of them are good for protection and grounding while others are best for enhancing connection with spirit and opening the third eye.

Working with a variety of stones and crystals is highly recommended since they all have very different vibrations and meanings. There are hundreds and thousands of various stones and so you may have to enjoy doing a little digging and research to find the best fit for your personal needs.

Try an experiment to find the right stones and crystals: Find a local shop in your area that specializes in selling stones and crystals. While in the shop, use your dominant magick hand (it might not be your dominant writing hand) and hover over the stones you feel drawn to. Let your intuition be your guide. If you feel "pulled" toward a stone, pick it up and notice how it feels. If you can sense a strong energy in it through the palm of your hand, then that stone or crystal is resonating with your vibration and will be good for you to work with.

Everything in your tool kit is a way for you to gain more connection to the greater energies and spirits of the world around you. As you work with these tools, look for the ways that they make you feel energetically attuned to what you are working on. Sometimes, you may resonate more with the fire element and may desire more candlelight in your practice; other times, you may have a need to bring more Earthly items from nature into your casting or take yourself out into the woods to do your rituals.

All of the elements play a major role in your Wicca work and so developing relationships with these tools is of vital importance. The work you do with the energy of nature brings a deeper and closer connection to yourself and all of the energies that are here to help you and guide you on your path. Work on building the tool kit that feels like you and enjoy practicing your rituals with your sacred and magical elements.

Setting Up Your Altar

An Altar is a space of devotion to something. It can be anything you want it to be and creating your altar is the artistic expression of your magik and your practice. We all need a place in our homes that reflects our most important desires and passions as well as our thoughts and expectations. An altar is a perfect way to create a physical manifestation of your spiritual journey.

There are no rules to setting up your altar and often times, it will change with you as you grow and evolve. It takes on the life you are living as you add and subtract things from it based on the intentions and practices you are doing.

Altars are a reflection of who you are and what you are praying to and so while you develop your own altar, be clear about how it shows off what you are choosing to align with at all times. It needs to be a place that has a flow and an energy of harmony and balance. It may be necessary for you to tend to your altar daily or frequently to maintain its energy and ability to attract abundance into your life.

Your altar should be in a place in your home where it cannot be disturbed easily by others and can be easily seen by you so that you are always alive to it. Many people put altars where anyone can see them and that is perfectly okay; it doesn't need to be hidden; it only needs space to exist undisturbed by anyone but you.

The altar of your choice can be on a bookshelf, in a cabinet, on top of your dresser, hanging on the wall, etc. It is up to you to choose the right place for your altar to exist. Once you have found the proper location, you can acquire the items you need to create it and decorate it.

Often times, people will use a cloth to lay out on the surface of wherever it will sit. It could be something small, like a scarf or a handkerchief or it could be something more meaningful, like a piece of heirloom lace from your Grandmother. You don't have to use a cloth at all, but if you choose to, make sure it is something that reflects the overall energy of your altar.

Next, you can start bringing in objects to help you align with your spiritual path and purpose. Many people place sculptures or figurines of their favored gods and goddesses, others may use paintings, pictures, or photographs to set out as an homage to a particular deity. Anything goes really and it all depends on what you like and what you are wanting to focus on.

Another approach is to just use the items from your tool kit. You can place these items on the altar and dedicate this space to your sacred rituals so that your tools are always resting on your altar. Essentially, building an altar for your magical tools. Bringing focus to these items through the display on an altar will remind you of the importance of working with this magik and will help you continue to honor your Wiccan practice. When you are opening your energies to work with your tools, you can start by lighting candles on your altar, burning some incense or smudging the altar and starting your rituals in this way.

Your altar is basically a display of your internal magical self. It is a reflection of your power and your curiosity to ask questions about the great unknown and to worship the energy of all things in this world. Bring to your altar anything that is resonating with you at the time. You may decide to decorate it with fresh cut flowers and let them wilt and dry to illustrate the idea of life and death.

You may also want to collect items from your nature walks to devote the altar to Mother Earth. It can also be a place that changes with every Wiccan holiday celebration making your altar a devotion to the seasons and rhythms of the Earth.

Don't be afraid to alter your altar. It can transform with you as you grow and it will need to be tended to the way you tend to yourself. Treat it like a living thing and as an expression of yourself. Whatever water you keep on your altar, if any, needs to be clean and pure; don't let it get dirty and stagnant as that will be a sign showing you that you are neglecting your altar and your spiritual practice.

Tend to it and allow it to be a consistently transforming part of your life that invokes a deeper spiritual reflection of your journey.

Asking the Gods/Goddesses for Support

Whether you are looking for guidance from the gods and goddesses of Pagan ritual or not, letting yourself be open to their assistance and guidance is a good way to bond with the energies of all things as you work with your Wiccan practices. You may not have a particular deity that you work with or devote your altar to but as you are preparing your rituals, it is a good idea to let the universal energies know that you are ready to tap in and find help if it is offered as you cast your spells and perform your rituals.

All you have to do is say the following words as you light the candles on your altar and burn your incense:

"I am opening the lights of all life to the energy of all things. I ask for guidance, support, and protection from the Great Mother and Father and all offerings from the spirits and deities of all life. I am open to receive your love, light, and warmth as I progress in my ritual. So mote it be."

You can change the wording to be anything that feels right for you based on what energies you want to call in to help. You may be more inclined to practice fairy magic or to work with the animal kingdom of spirit guides. You may also desire to connect with your ancestors as you begin your rituals and spell castings. All of these ways of connecting to that work will help you, so make sure it is in alignment with how your individual Wiccan practice is for you.

Change the wording of the above message to reflect your practice but keep the message the same. Stating that you are open to receive help and guidance is a very powerful tool of connection. Maintaining a desire to only work with the energies of light and love is an important factor because it declares that you are wanting to work with the higher vibrations and that you don't want to call on anything harmful or low energy like a trickster spirit or energy who may not be as helpful as other energies will be.

Opening yourself to all of this will help you concentrate even better on what your intentions are and what you are wanting to accomplish with your spells. Relax, ask for support, and give thanks to all the energies that come to provide you with help along your path.

Casting Your Circle

You don't have to use your altarpiece to cast your circle. You may be out in the woods when you need to cast and will be far away from your altar. It might be also that you just utilize your altar to store your magical tools between casting and won't need to involve it in your Wicca work; however, you may find that you feel more grounded in your practices if you start by connecting with the energy of your altar before casting your circle. It is really up to you how you choose to work with your own energy and magical tools.

Why do you cast a circle and what does it even mean? When you are invoking the energies all around you and connect your own energy to the spiritual plane, you need to have an opening and closing of intention and protection. It is a helpful way for you to have clarity and focus while you are performing rituals and casting spells but it also serves as an intentional centering of your energy and attachment to your spiritual self. Casting is almost like a meditation to get you engaged with your work.

The meaning of casting a circle in your preparation is also to align you with the four directions and the four elements. Each way you travel is represented by your circle and each element of the life spark is represented to connect you to your full purpose and potential. It is a meaningful acknowledgment of your journey when you cast a circle and it brings into focus that which helps you succeed on your path: the directions and the elements.

Remember to create a space that feels healthy and balanced for you while you practice. It is best to do it away from where others will interrupt or disturb you. The following steps will help you cast your circle of intention and protection.

1. If you are working near your altar and you want to include it into your ritual, you can begin by lighting candles on the altar and lighting your smudge stick to cleanse the energy of the altar and your body.

2. Facing the north, say the following words: "I call upon the energy of the north. Welcome to this circle of light. And so it is."

3. Facing the east, say the following words: "I call upon the energy of the east. Welcome to this circle of light. And so it is."

4. Facing the south, say the following words: "I call upon the energy of the south. Welcome to this circle of light. And so it is."

Facing the west, say the following words: "I call upon the energy of the west. Welcome to this circle of light. And so it is."

**NOTE:* You have creative freedom to change the wording of these phrases. They are a simplified version of what you can say to announce the calling of the four directions into your circle and you may find as you advance and feel more creative with your practice that you will want to add some information to how you call upon the directions.

5. Once you have called on the directions, you can now invite the elements to wherever you are sitting. You may keep your elements placed on the altar or you may wish to set them out on the table you are sitting at or on the ground if you are sitting at that level. You can use specific tools and objects for this part and if you can, lay the corresponding element in the directional position it is aligned with. For example, for your

earth element, place your dish of salt or soil to the north.

6. Set your earth element in the position of the north (wherever you are sitting) and say the following words: "I call upon the energy of earth as I cast my circle of protection and power. Welcome to this circle of light. And so it is."

7. Repeat Step 7 as you did with the directions in Steps 2-5, laying out an object or representation for each element. East is air; south is fire; west is water. You can use a smoking incense or smudge stick for air or you can place bird feathers in this position. A candle works for the position of the south and fire, and a dish of clean, clear water works for the west.

8. Alternatives for these items would be crystals or stones that would resonate with the directional energies; a stone or crystal for each direction representing the elements.

The final step of the circle casting can be a personal declaration, like the following: "*I awaken to the energies of the four directions and the four elements and cast this circle of protect and light with their help and guidance as I work with their energies. So mote it be."*

**NOTE: The phrases 'So mote it be' and 'and so it is' are saying the exact same thing. It is the energy of stating 'and this is real'. Saying it at the end of an intentional phrase is a very powerful energetic assignment for whatever magick you are performing. Either one works well and can be used interchangeably.

You are now on your way to delving more deeply into the ritual and spell casting that you are choosing. Get comfortable with how you like to cast your circle and repeat it the same way every time. Casting a circle of power and protection is a ritual in and of itself and your personal circle casting should be unique to you. Build your own version of casting a circle from the steps above and have fun with it!

Spells, Rituals, Intentions

The next step in the process of a typical spell or ritual is the actual spell work or ritual work that aligns you with your intentions. Remember: it is important to have clear intentions before going in, so before you cast your circle, ask yourself: what is my magical purpose today?

Once you have clarity about what you are wanting to achieve or focus on, you may want to design your ritual or spell from your own personal idea of how it should go or you can use already existing spells and craft work that feel natural and good for what you are wanting to accomplish. There are tons of spells online, in books, all over, that can help you choose the best way for you to align with your craft work.

Much of what you will be doing in this step is clearly detailing and stating your intentions to create the energy of life around it. It may include herbs and other items that support your intention. If you are celebrating a holiday or a specific god or goddess, you will be working with those items and energies specifically to enhance your ritual or spell.

Words are important and you may need to write down ahead of time the words you want to share once you have opened a circle. Preparing for your ritual or spell is just as important as executing it. Prior to opening your circle, write down the words for your spell on a piece of paper. Gather the herbs you wish to include in your circle, or the relics and objects that will be meaningful to you.

There are so many unique possibilities for how you can invoke your own powerful magik and let it be known to the energies of all that surrounds you. The following steps are simple ideas and clues for how you can get started with creating your ritual and spell. Remember that practicing Wicca is a creative and artistic experience and there really isn't a wrong way to do it. You can use the following steps to help get you started with building a spell and/or ritual.

1. Set your intention. Write it on paper, on leaves, on stones or pieces of wood to burn, on anything magical.

2. Gather your ingredients. You may be working with herbal remedies that support your intention. Make a bouquet of them to dry on your altar. Collect the stones, crystals and any other earth elements that feel appropriate and place them where they feel best. You may want to collect sacred water from a waterfall or a river that feels magical to you.

3. After casting your circle of protection and power, you can now begin your ritual with your objects and intentions. Using your written intentions as a declaration is a wonderful way to open yourself up to the energy of what you are wanting to accomplish. Don't just write it on the paper or the leaves; read it aloud so that you can feel the words come out of your mouth with sound and release the words into your circle.

4. Use your candles, incense and crystals, or other ritual objects to set intentions and make declarations as well. For example: if you are

using fire magic, you may have chosen a certain number of colored candles that correspond with the energy you are wanting to invoke. As you light each candle you can say, *"As I light this candle, I welcome the power of fire to bless my ritual and invoke the passion of firelight to aid me on my path."*

**NOTE: Everything you do carries energy and intention, so even when you are lighting a candle, make declarations about what you are doing out loud so that the energy is clear in your ritual.

5. Use the same concept from Step 4 with your other ritual or spell casting elements. For example: if you have sacred river water to add to your ritual, as you pour it into a chalice or a bowl you can say something like: *"As this water flows into this cup, let it flow through me with intention and energy to fulfill my purpose. And so it is!"*

6. *After incorporating all of your ingredients for your spell you can recite, or speak aloud, your words of intention and incantation. Let's say you are casting a spell for prosperity. All you have to say is*: "Here on this day, I summon the life force energy of prosperity. The candle will burn night and day to align me with the fortune I seek. Water will flow in this chalice until prosperity

comes to me. Smoke I will burn every day and night to welcome the gift of abundance. Salt I will shake onto these coins to gain more of what I seek. Prosperity! And so it is!"

Any spells and rituals that you do will be fun, unique, and specific to the cause of the work you are doing. Once you have a basic feeling for how to open a circle and bring forth your intentions in your magical practice, you will find the freedom to explore more of the possibilities of finding and creating your own spells and rituals.

Even if you find popular spells online or in other books, you can always build onto or alter these spells to fit your needs. No harm will come to you if you make some changes to already existing spells. Wicca is a creative practice and all it needs is your devotion to the light of your truth and your inner knowing as you walk the path of Wicca.

Closing Your Circle

Closing your circle is as simple as opening it. All you have to do is pay respect and gratitude to the elements and to the directions. You may want to face each direction again to ask the directions to comfort you on your path as you allow your spell to take effect.

You can also connect with the elements you have in your space and carefully return them to their altar space as a way of creating closure with them. Here are a few steps to help you close your circle, as you opened it:

1. Thank each element by addressing it directly. *Ex:* Thank you to the earth that grounds me (sprinkle salt or soil into your hands and rub them together, letting the salt/soil fall away natural). Thank you to the air that blows me forward on my journey (snuff out the smudge stick). Thank you to the fire the lights my way (blow out candle). Thank you to the water that cleanses and purifies (dip fingers in water and flick on your altar or on your own face).

2. Stand up or point your energy in the direction of each of the four directions to thank them for their presence, similar to the way you did it with the elements in Step 1. All you have to do is offer gratitude and move through each direction, closing the circle the way it started.

3. Alternative: You can combine Steps 1 and 2 and close the circle by thanking each direction and the corresponding element simultaneously.

4. A final thank you can be expressed to the Great Mother and the Father or whichever gods/goddesses you have invoked for your ritual.

5. The final words: "And so it is!" or "So mote it be!"

Accepting Your True Power

Wicca is a beautiful, fun and magical way to connect with your true power and the energy of all life around you. It has a way of asking you to be present and to identify your whole being and the nature of what you are seeking with a mindful appreciation of nature and all of her energies.

One of the most profound lessons of Wicca and other Pagan practices is that it is a way for you to creatively explore yourself and your inner power as you transform and grow. The best way for you to approach rituals and casting spells is to trust your own inner knowing about how the spell should go and what ways it can unfold.

You will find a wide range of variations for one specific intention or spell, because there isn't a wrong way to cast. As long as you are upholding the Wiccan Rede, then anything goes, essentially. As you continue to work with your own spell work and rituals, remember to honor your power above all else. Devotions to the Earth Mother and all of the other gods and goddesses are equally important to the devotion of your own magical powers and truths.

Have fun inventing your own spells and create your own *grimoire*! A grimoire is simply a book of magic spells and invocations and you can make your own at any time as you see fit. Every spell you cast can be written down, step by step in your own book of magic that is specific to you and the traditions or beliefs you choose to follow. Working on your own grimoire is a special way of devoting yourself to your path of magic and having a reference to your own book of spell work can help you in the future when you want to repeat or enhance spells that you have already created and performed.

It is very traditional for a witch to make his or her own grimoire and so while you are opening yourself to your Wiccan experience, get a notebook and begin a journal of your recipes and incantations so that you can refer to and use them later. It is a helpful way to trust in your own magick and true power.

Spell for New Friendships

Whether you've just moved to a new area and don't know many people yet, or your social life simply needs an overhaul, this quick spell brings new people into your life to form friendships with if you so choose.

It's best done during a waxing moon, but if you've got an upcoming social encounter that you'd like to put some magical energy into, by all means, don't hold off just because the moon is waning.

You will need:

- 1 small rose quartz, clear quartz, carnelian, or lapis lazuli stone

- 1 yellow spell or votive candle

- Lavender essential oil

Instructions:

- Anoint the candle with the oil.

Place the stone in your dominant hand, palm upward, and lay your other palm on top.

Clasp your hands together, close your eyes, and visualize yourself surrounded by positive people who are fun and comforting to be around.

When you've captured this feeling, take a deep breath, exhale, and open your eyes.

Place the stone in front of the candle and then light the wick as you say these words:

"Friendships new and true, let our kindred souls unite. "

Carry the stone with you whenever you leave the house, and leave it where you will see it when you are home.

Charm for Attracting Quality Relationships

As a culinary spice, coriander has a warm, fragrant, slightly nutty flavor. But not everyone knows that coriander is actually the seed of the herb known as cilantro.

Interestingly, the seed and the leaf taste nothing alike. This dual nature is reflected in the magical uses of coriander, which include both attracting love and guarding against unwanted energies.

The seed is used in love spells, aphrodisiac potions, and for making peace between quarreling people, as well as for exorcism and protection of the home. And because it's readily available in the spice aisle of most grocery stores, it's a great herb to work with for beginning kitchen Witches.

This spell draws on both the attractive and protective qualities of coriander for a balanced approach to attracting new potential partners into your life.

This is particularly good for those who seem to have no trouble attracting admirers, but plenty of trouble in the relationships that develop. With the energy of coriander, people who are ultimately no good for you will not make it into your sphere of awareness, while people who present a positive, healthy, compatible match will have a clear path to you.

Adding rose quartz to the mix enhances the positive vibration of the spell. Be sure to get whole seeds rather than coriander powder, since you'll be carrying the herb with you.

You will need:

- 13 whole coriander seeds

- 1 small rose quartz

- 1 small drawstring bag or piece of cloth

- 1 red or pink ribbon

- 1 work candle (for atmosphere—optional)

- Instructions:

- Light the candle, if using.

Arrange the coriander seeds in a circle around the rose quartz.

Close your eyes and visualize the feeling of being completely at peace with a partner who loves you for exactly who you are.

When you have a lock on this feeling, open your eyes, focus on the rose quartz, and say the following (or similar) words:

"I draw to be nothing less than healthy, balanced love."

Now collect the coriander seeds, placing them one at a time into the drawstring bag or cloth. (It's best to start with the seed at the southern-most part of the circle and move clockwise.)

Add the rose quartz, close the bag or cloth, and secure with the ribbon.

Bring the charm with you whenever you're feeling like taking a chance on love—especially when you go out in public.

Romance Attraction Smudge

This is a fun, simple ritual for enhancing the atmosphere in your home or any space where you'd like to encourage romance!

You will need:

- 1 red candle

- A sprig of dried lavender or lavender-only smudge stick

- Rose essential oil (optional)

- 1 feather (optional)

Instructions:

Anoint the candle with a drop or two of the rose oil, if using. Wipe away any excess oil from your fingers, and then light the candle.

Ignite the lavender sprig or smudge stick from the candle flame as you say the following (or similar) words:

"Loving lavender, creative fire,
charge this space with love's desire."

Starting at a point in the northern part in the room, move in a clockwise circle, fanning the lavender smoke with the feather (if using) or your hand, so that it spreads throughout the room as much as possible. If you like, you can repeat the words of power above as a chant as you go.

Leave the lavender to burn out on its own in a fire-proof dish, if possible—otherwise, you can extinguish it gently in a potted plant or bowl of sand.

Stellar First Date Confidence Charm

If you're the type who gets nervous before meeting a potential love interest for the first time, this spell is for you.

Simply carry the charm with you in your pocket or purse—you may want to enclose it in a drawstring bag or cloth if you're carrying it with other items to keep it intact.

Keep in mind that the focus here is on your own confidence and sense of self-love *no matter what the* other person is like. If you have a good time, no matter what the outcome, then the spell has been a success.

You will need:

- One pink or white ribbon, about seven inches

- One little piece of carnelian or tiger's eye

- Sea salt

- One work candle (optional)

- One little drawstring bag or piece of cloth (optional)

Instructions:

Light the candle, if using.

Layout the ribbon on your altar or workspace.

Create a circle of sea salt around the ribbon—this will concentrate the energy of the spell around the charm.

Place the stone on the ribbon, and say the following (or similar) words:

"My confidence radiates from within I am comfortable in my own skin. This meeting of souls will be a pleasure. I charm this stone for extra measure."

"

Tie the ribbon gently around the stone and secure it with a knot.

Now go out and have fun meeting someone new!

Ritual Bath for a Blind Date

Whether you're on a blind date set up by a friend, or taking the plunge in the world of online dating, it can be nerve-wracking to meet someone new.

This spell makes it nearly impossible not to have a good time, by sublimating nervousness and promoting self-confidence, which will improve the energy of the encounter no matter what the outcome. Indeed, you will enjoy yourself even if it's clear by the end that there won't be a second date!

Himalayan salt is a wonderful relaxant, but it can be potent and induce sleepiness, especially if you don't use it regularly. Therefore, if you're taking this bath right before the date, you may want to opt for the sea salt.

The herbs can be sprinkled loosely if you have a mesh catch-all drain for your tub. Otherwise, place them in a teabag or a thin washcloth to keep them from spreading out into the water.

You will need:

- One tsp. to one tbsp. hibiscus

- One tsp. to one tbsp. chamomile

- One tsp. to one. tbsp. coltsfoot or red clover

- Two to three tbsp. Himalayan salt or sea salt

- Five drops of lavender essential oil

- One citrine, aventurine, or tiger's eye

- Candle(s) for atmosphere

Instructions:

Run the bath until the tub is a quarter of the way full, and add the salt.

When the tub is halfway full, place the crystal of your choice in the water, and add the oil.

When the bath is almost full, add the herbs.

Light the candle(s), turn off any artificial lighting in the bathroom, and climb in.

Relax and consciously release any anxiety you may be feeling about meeting this new person. Also, release any attachments you may be feeling to the desired outcome.

Stay in the bath for at least 20 minutes. If you can, remain in the tub while draining the water, as the energy of the herbs and crystal tends to have a stronger effect that way.

Bring the crystal with you on the date, and have a good time!

Relationship Potential Divine "Forecast"

For single people, getting to know a new potential love interest can be exciting, but also confusing.

Even though you may seem to "click" with this person, you're still operating in an atmosphere where there's far more unknown information than known. It can be hard to avoid wondering whether it will work out in the way you're hoping for, and easy to get caught up in over-analyzing even the smallest of details.

Perhaps you're wondering if the person is "too good to be true," or worried that you might jump into something too quickly. Or you may just be trying to talk yourself out of a potentially great relationship simply because it will require you to leave your comfort zone. Maybe it's a little bit of all of the above?

The problem, of course, is that over-thinking it actually gets in the way of your ability to see the situation clearly and can create more confusion, rather than less. This spell can help you get a sense of whether your new prospect has enough romantic potential to be worth putting further mental energy into.

You may get a simple, definitive *yes* or *no*, but you may also get more information that helps you come to your own decision about it or a signal that for now you just need to stay open and detached from any particular outcome. Whatever your "forecast" turns out to be, this spell will get the energy moving from a place of stuckness toward a place of resolution, by helping you get out of your own way!

Any of the three crystals below work well for this spell, but if you happen to have all of these and are looking to choose one, here are some finer energetic points to consider for your particular situation:

• *Malachite* is particularly appropriate if your current confusion or concern stems primarily from a prior relationship experience.

• *Quartz* is a good all-purpose intuition booster and helps clear out inner turmoil.

• *Amethyst* helps to dispel illusions and keep "obsessive thinking" in check.

You will need:

• One little to average-sized amethyst, quartz crystal, or malachite

• One little strand of paper

• One scented candle (optional)

Instructions:

Light the candle, if using.

Spend some time getting grounded and centered. Let go of any actual thoughts around the person for the time being.

Write the person's name on the strip of paper, and ask for any and all illusions you may have about the person to be cleared away. (Don't ask specific questions, or your mental energy will muddy up the spell.)

You may want to say the following (or similar) words:

"Infinite intelligence of the Universe,
please light the path that I am meant to see,
with regard to [name of person] and me."

Fold the paper enough times so that it more or less fits underneath the crystal, and place it on your altar with the crystal on top.

When you go to bed, place the crystal (and paper) underneath your pillow. You will likely receive further information in your dreams, but don't worry if this doesn't happen—information of some kind will come to you in your waking life within the next 48 hours.

Choosing Peace in Tough Situations

At some point in our lives, we all face enormous challenges that we know we can do nothing to control. It may be that a loved one is facing a serious illness, or it may even be a major world event causing chaos in your life.

It's always fine to work magic for whatever influence you may be able to have on the outcome of a situation, but this can be difficult to do from a place of empowerment when you're feeling personally affected, which can negate the energy of the spell.

In times like these, you need to take care of yourself first before you can help anyone else.

This spell is best worked for an hour or so before going to bed. If you prefer to let spell candles burn all the way down on their own, you'll need to place it in a sink before going to sleep!

Otherwise, you can gently extinguish the candle and repeat the spell on successive nights until the candle is spent.

This spell is really meant to be personalized as much as you wish. Put on meditative music, brew chamomile tea, stretch your limbs, take a hot bath, and/or do anything else that helps you relax. The more energetically "prepped" you are for this spell, the more powerful it will be.

You will need:

- Peace of Mind Oil blend

- 1 white candle

- Meditative music (optional)

Instructions:

Put on the music, if using, and take any other measures to calm yourself as much as you can.

Sit quietly and take a few deep breaths. Anoint your pulse points and the candle with the oil.

Close your eyes and take a few more deep breaths, clearing your mind as much as possible.

When you feel ready, open your eyes and light the candle, while saying the following (or similar) words:

I release this burden to my higher power and turn my attention to balance and rest. So, let it be.

Sit and gaze at the candle flame for several moments, keeping your mind as quiet as possible and your focus on the light.

"Spare Key" Spell for Spiritual Connection

Although we usually think of other people in the context of "relationship," we also have a relationship with our "higher power"—or whatever your personal term is for the force that moves through you when working magic. This spell focuses on strengthening that relationship, which is ultimately the foundation from which all human relationships stem.

While it may be becoming less common in today's world, it has long been the custom of many households to keep a spare key just outside the home, whether under the doormat, in a potted plant, or some other hidden location. This is done as both a backup in the case of lost keys and as a way of allowing relatives or friends access when the homeowner is away.

This spell draws on the energies of wisdom and trust that are inherent to this custom, as a way of honoring the benevolent forces working for you in the unseen realms.

By blessing and burying a key outside near your home (or in a potted plant indoors, if necessary) you are signaling to your higher power—whether it be a deity, a guardian spirit, or simply the benevolent energy of the Universe—that you welcome their presence and assistance in your home and in your life, no matter where you may be at any given moment.

It is also a way of reminding yourself that should you temporarily lose your connection to your spiritual center, you will always be able to find your way back in.

Depending on whether the crime is a factor in your neighborhood, you may feel comfortable using an actual spare key to your home, but any metal key will work for this spell.

Some people like to use a gold key to represent God and/or a silver key to represent the Goddess (using two keys is perfectly fine).

You will need:

- 1 key

- 1 white candle

Instructions:

Hold the key in your hands while meditating quietly for several minutes.

Focus on that feeling of being truly connected to your true self and your higher power.

When you feel ready, light the candle and say the following (or similar) words:

"[Name of deity/spirit/higher power], you are welcome now and always in my home and my heart. Let this key represent your access, and mine, to my highest self, from this day forward."

Pass the key through the candle flame very quickly three times (in order to protect your fingers, don't give it any time to become hot).

Then bury it at least 6 inches down into the earth outside your home, or in the soil of a large potted plant.

Chapter 5 : Herbal Magic: Rituals and Spells

There are thousands and thousands of magical rituals and spells that you can incorporate into your herbal magic practice. This chapter will give you some highlights of things that you can do to utilize herbs for casting spells, brewing potions and a variety of other things as well. In the last chapter, you read about more of the healing brews and potions, but always remember that they are no less magical than the recipes you are about to read. All of your herbal craft work has a magic to it and these rituals and spells are just another exciting layer to your Wicca Herbal Magic practice.

Magical Tea Infusion for Any Kind of Potion or Brew

So many of these potions are really just a simple tea. The last chapter had a few examples of some healing tea potions to help you in times of sickness and health and you can infuse more magic into any of those brews with this simple Tea Infusion Ritual. Use it daily, for any tea you want to brew. The magical energy that you use to charge all of your spells and remedies will bring you a fulfilling enrichment from the inside out.

Instructions for Making and Enjoying a Magical Tea (Infusion)

Follow these steps to empower your tea:

1. While steeping the potion, envision yourself covered light (choose the color based on what magical effect you are needing. Ex: green for healing; pink for love; orange for power, etc.)

2. While pouring and drinking the potion, visualize that same colored light coming from the liquid.

3. After drinking, see the light radiating from within you, flowing through your whole body and then out into the world around you

4. See it reach towards the sky (as above) and go down into the earth (so below), extending your will and desire into the universe.

5. You can say a mantra or affirmation for your Tea Spell while you drink and envision the light.

Making a Magical Tincture

You have already read instructions for making a tincture in Chapter 3, and this spell and ritual will help you infuse your tinctures with a charge of energy and magical intention or purpose. Every time you shake your jar of herbal alcohol potion (twice daily for one month) you will infuse it with the magic energy you need through this tincture charging spell.

Spell and Ritual to Charge Your Tinctures

You will need the following:

- 1 green candle- represents herbal spirits

- 1 white candle- honoring spirit and magic

- 1 candle to charge the tincture- the color chosen depends on the spell you are working

- mixing bowl – glass or stainless steel, no plastic

- Herbs and alcohol for the tincture (or alcohol substitute)

- 2 Mason jars

- Cheesecloth

1. Create a triangle with your candles on your altar, or wherever you are performing your ritual. Put the white candle at the top point of the triangle, farthest from you and the green and other candle at the base points of the triangle. The white candle point directs energy from you and out into the Universe.

2. Place the bowl in the center of the triangle of candles on your altar. Your herbs and alcohol (or substitute) should be near to where you are working, but not yet in the bowl.

3. As you light the white candle, state the following: "For the power of the spirit"

4. As you light the white candle, state the following: "For the herbal spirits"

5. Depending on the final colored candle and your needs for this tincture spell, light the candle and state your purpose as you did with the other two candles.

6. With each herb you are using for your tincture, you will pre-measure your ingredients before you start your ritual. After lighting the candles, you will take each herb measurement, one at a time, and as you place it in the bowl on the altar you will offer a blessing of gratitude and state your need for that particular herb.

7. You will repeat this ritual for each herb you put into the bowl, one by one. As you add each herb, stir the mixture clockwise to incorporate them together. Clockwise is the direction for increasing or bringing something to you in this practice. Counterclockwise would be the decreasing or removal of excess of something in your life.

8. After all, herbs are added and stirred, place your hand over the bowl and state your magical purpose and intention.

9. Depending on your need, and likely corresponding to the color candle you have chosen for your specific spell, imagine and visualize that color of light coming out of your hands and into the herb mixture on the altar, charging it with colorful light. (Ex: love = pink light; money = green light, etc.)

10. Away from the lit candles, pour your herbs into your mason jar and add the alcohol. Secure the jars with lid.

11. Taking the mixing bowl off of the altar, put the jar of herb and alcohol mixture in its place in the center of the candle triangle. Leave the jar in this place until the candles have all finished burning.

12. Once the candles have burned out, you can move your sacred tincture to a darker place to cure. It can be somewhere on your altar covered with a cloth, or in a cupboard.

13. As you shake the tincture, focus on your energy on all planes, body, mind, spirit. You can come up with your own chant to say as you shake, but here is one example of what you might say, every time you shake your jar: "Herbal potion, magic brew, I shake your powers, releasing true. Giving power, making light, magic set, in tincture right."

14. You will need to shake the jar twice a day for at least a month and will want to repeat your words and visualize your intentions as you do.

15. After the month has passed, you can strain your liquid through the cheesecloth and remove all of the herbal plant fibers. You can then dilute it with distilled water, if desired, and keep bottled and store for magical use!

Spell and Ritual to Charge Your Bath

There are a variety of herbs that you can use to make a ritual bath. A majority of the herbs that you will put in your bath will most likely need to be in a sachet, or a larger tea bag so that they don't clog your drain when you let the water out of the bath. You can also add larger blossoms and petals to the water, essentially making a giant infusion to relax your body in.

Ritual baths are incredibly healing to the body and the spirit and if you are working with magic and herbal remedy, then this spell will hell you to charge the herbs and charms for your bath experience so that you are floating on the highest vibration of magic possible.

You will need the following:

- An assortment of herbs (depends on your spell work)

- Sea or Epsom Salt

- Sachet to hold herbs

- Essential oils (optional)

- Mixing bowl

- Candles (choose the colors based on your spell's needs)

- Flower petals and heads (dry or fresh)

- Smudge stick

On your altar, set your candles either in a triangle or arch. Make the point of the triangle or arch farthest from you. (You can also do this ritual on the kitchen table if your altar isn't big enough).

1. Place the mixing bowl in the center of the candles on your altar.

2. Light each candle, invoking the energy of the candle magic you are asking for in your spell. It will depend on your intentions and your purpose as well as the color of the candle you have chosen.

3. Once the candles are lit, slowly add your herbs to the mixing bowl, one by one. Each time you add a new herb, stir the mixture. You will want to stir clockwise to add to or gain something from your

ritual bath, and counterclockwise to purge, remove or release something as you bathe. It depends on your spell.

4. You can add fresh or dried herbs, salt, magical powder, essential oils, and anything else appropriate to your spell, stirring in the correct direction with a sacred tool, each time you add something new.

5. After you have mixed everything together, light your smudge stick and allow it to smoke. Once it has smoke flowing, swirl the smoke into the mixing bowl in the direction you have chosen it needs to go and say the following words:

"Herbal mixture, green goddess light, come into my bath tonight. Mix with water, purify. Sacred magic, lift my light."

Play around with words and phrases that are pertinent to your spell. **You can also bring your smudge stick into the bath with you later to smudge the water before getting in.

1. Place your hands over the mixture in the bowl and visualize the color of light that is appropriate to your spell, coming through your hands and into the mixture. State any words that will invoke the energy needed in your sacred bath ritual.

2. Once charged, you can begin to put the herbal mixture into the sachets, tying them off and preparing them for the bath.

3. Remove the bowl from the altar and place the sachets in the center of the candles on the altar or workspace. You can leave them there for as long as you feel it is needed, or until the candles burn out.

4. Your bath sachets are now charged with your magic and you can perform the ritual. As you draw your bath, stir your water in the same direction you stirred your herbs in the mixing bowl and incant some words to let the water know your intentions and purpose. As the water spins in the tub, add your sacred herbs to the water to allow them time to steep.

5. Light some candles and smudge the tub. You can smudge before you draw the bath or after; it is up to you.

6. Add some fresh or dried rose petals, or other flower heads to the bath. You can also add some drop of charged essential oils (you can use the same candlelight work and visualization charging on your bottles of essential oils).

7. While in your bath, let the herbs work their magic on your spirit. Visualize what you are trying to invoke or manifest through this spell and let yourself relax into the possibilities.

8. When you drain the water, ask it to carry your magic forward into the universe and to bring your intentions into life and all reality.

Herbal Love Potion Spell

Who doesn't want some extra love in their life? Everyone is looking for a little love and when you work with the energies and herbs that can promote those relationships, emotions, and experiences, you are giving a serious boost to your love experience.

With any spell, it all comes down to specifics and exactly what you are trying to invoke or manifest. Love spells can be anything from drawing your true love to you, to increasing sexual passions, to promoting a deeper bond and marriage partnership.

Every spell needs your specific intentions and purposes and so it will be up to you to modify any ritual, potion, brew or energy to be comparable to what your desires are.

For this Herbal love potion spell, it will be a simple energetic approach to allowing an increase of love power in your life. Whether it is to enhance your already existing relationships or to open yourself to new ones, this spell is designed to increase the energy of love's passion and flow into your life.

You will need the following:

- Roses

- Rose petals

- Lavender

- Cinnamon

- Jasmine

- Peppermint

- Chamomile

- Rosemary

**NOTE: Herbs may be fresh or dry

- Mixing bowl

- Pink and Gold candles (3-5)

- Incense (cinnamon, jasmine, or rose)

This simple infusion is like any other tea you might make, but in order to charge and infuse it with your intentions, there are a few extra steps to help you make it a truly magical love potion. For the ingredients, be creative with how much of each you want to use. Depending on your personality and personal likes, you may want more jasmine in your infusion than roses. You'll probably only need a pinch of cinnamon and a smaller dose of the chamomile and lavender because of their strong sedative qualities.

1. Begin this ritual the same way you started your last one (see Spell and Ritual to Charge Your Bath), by setting your candles on your altar or

workspace, either in a triangle or arch, with the top or point farthest away from you.

2. Place your mixing bowl in the center of the candle arrangement and light the candles stating: "Magic fire, candlelight, I invoke your power and wisdom right. Love is life and mine is true, I choose to love and bring it through."

3. Once the candles are lit, light your incense on the altar. You can make a statement at this time to invoke the powers of love through the aromatics you are burning.

4. Ready to add the herbs, you can start adding each one by one. Communicate what each herb or flower means to you in the light of love. Each one may have a different essence and energy for you, and it is different for everyone. Let your intuition guide your thoughts and words and speak the magic of each herb as you add it.

5. Every time you add a new element to the bowl, stir it clockwise, to increase love and making it bigger in your life.

6. Once your magical love herbs are all mixed together in the bowl, send your purpose and intentions into the love potion. You can use creative visualizations, spoken words, and you can even invoke the deity and goddess of love, Venus to help empower your potion.

7. Let the mixture sit by the candlelight until the candle burn out. You may wish to relight some of your love incense to keep the energy potent and aromatic.

8. While you wait for your love potion to charge by candle magic, eat some love foods, like pomegranates, apples, figs, and berries. Envision the love power you are wanting to invoke while you eat these treats.

9. After the candles have burned out, you can now use the herbs to make an herbal infusion to drink. You may want to save some of those love foods to enjoy while you sip your tea.

10. Adjust the quantities as preferred and add the love potion to boiling water and allow to steep for up to 10 and no more than 15 minutes before drinking.

11. Enjoy by a warm fire or in the loving sunlight, or even under the goddess moon.

12. You may also like to use these same herbs to create a sacred ritual love bath. You can blend the sacred bath and the love potion infusion into one magical night of love power to enhance your magical intentions.

Sun and Moon Charging Ritual

So much of the Wiccan practice is celebrating the cycles and rhythms of Mother Nature and all of the powerful energies aligned with those cycles. A great deal of the magic work that you do has an energy of intention that relates to the night and the day, the power of the sun and the moon.

A variety of spells and rituals are performed around these important cycles and energies and can have a potent energetic charge to any spell work or magical practice. The following ritual offers instructions on how to use the energy of the sun and/or the moon to charge your herbal potions, spells, and brews.

You will need the following:

- Herbs of your choice (fresh or dry- depending on the spell)

- Glass, wood, or steel mixing bowl (alternative: sacred cloth for rituals)

- Smudge stick

- Dry, safe place outdoors

- Moonlit night

- Sunny day

The process of this ritual is similar to other rituals. You may want to cast a circle of protection outside around your outdoor workspace or altar to create an intention. You can also use magical herbs and powders to sprinkle a circle around your workspace.

1. Bring the ingredients you need outside to the spot where you will be working.

2. Place the bowl there and you may light a candle and the smudge stick

3. Smudge the area around your temporary outdoor altar space, working in a clockwise direction,

since you are wanting to charge your herbs, or add the sun or moon power to them. This would be a good time to sprinkle your magic or protective herbs around the space.

4. Add the herbs of your choice to the bowl or cloth, on at a time if you are using more than one, stirring clockwise with each addition. You can burn your smudge stick at intervals as you stir as well. (If you are using a sacred cloth instead of a bowl for your herbs to lay out in the light, you can use your hand to spread the herbs around in a clockwise fashion, or sweeping motions)

5. As you add each herb, you can say some spell work words to invoke the energies of the herbs and declare your intention to charge them with the light of the sun or moon (you can choose both sun and moon and do an overnight into afternoon spell).

6. Place your hands over the herbs once they are incorporated together and envision the silver light of moonlight going into them, or the golden light of sunshine (or both depending on your spell).

7. If you feel a need to cover the herbs so they are not disturbed by animals or rain, try to find a glass lid that the light can get through and if possible, avoid plastics.

8. Leave the herbs on the outdoor altar for as long as you need the moonlight or the sunlight or both. It is advisable to let them charge for at least 5 hours and not more than 10, depending on the time of year and the daylight/ moonlight hours available.

9. Once you have finished with the charging ritual, you can close the circle, paying respects and gratitude to the sun and moon and bring your herbal potion back inside to be jarred and stored.

10. If you feel a need to refresh the moonlight/sunlight charge on this jar of herbs, you can just place the jar back outside in a second ritual as you see the need.

All of these rituals and spells can be modified, recreated and built upon based on your own practice and magical needs. All spells and rituals are a creative craft and art form, so don't be afraid to step outside of the box and peer through the kaleidoscope. There are so many possibilities for what you can do. Enjoy the fun of crafting your spells and rituals and watch your life transform in meaningful ways to help support the happiness, healing, and joy that comes from a magical life!

Chapter 6: Spells for Wealth

When witches cast spells for wealth, it may not always be spells for money, because real wealth can't always be measured in financial terms. And even if wealth comes your way, what is the true price? Asking for spells for wealth falls under the 'Be careful what you wish for' banner. Is it really in your best interests? You need to think these things through before you decide to cast spells for wealth.

And always remember this: Harm None. Another point to remember that your wealth spell should be cast for need, not for greed. Don't ask for wealth unless you really need it, or the magick won't work. With that in mind, here are some simple wealth spells that work.

Herbs of Prosperity

You may think having a pot of herbs in the home is nothing to do with spells, but consider this. First, you need to know which herbs have magickal properties, and what they are, and then you have to focus intent on the herb, and believe it will bring you wealth. So, have a small pot of basil, parsley, rosemary or thyme to bring prosperity to your home. Or more than one!

Bowl of Change

Place a bowl of change by the front door to keep money in your pocket. Add foreign coins and old, out of circulation coins to bring money into the home.

Mandrake Money

This is one for people with retail businesses. Wrap a large denomination note around a piece of mandrake root and secure with an elastic band. Keep it in your cash register and wait for your turnover to double. It will happen soon.

Abundance Candle Spell

Use the energy and power of the candle flame to draw wealth to you with this simple spell. You need:

- A green candle

- Cinnamon oil

- Vanilla oil

- A coin of large denomination

Carve the word 'Wealth' along the length of the candle with a sharp object – a craft knife, scalpel or toothpick would do it. Now use the oils to anoint the carved word. Place the coin in the candle holder, and then set the candle on top of it. Light the candle, and allow it to burn completely away.

When the candle has burned out, take the wax covered coin and keep it in a safe place to bring wealth to you.

The Self-Love Spell

This spell focuses on self-love and self-importance. It is very easy to accomplish, and it only takes about ten minutes. It is the perfect spell to start with if you want to continue on the path of love spells.

Ingredients needed:

- One birthday candle (pink or red is preferred, but since this spell is about you, specifically, use whatever candle calls to you)

- Essential oil (orange, rose, jasmine, or sandalwood)

- One rose quartz crystal

- One agate slice

- A pinch of Himalayan pink salt

Step 1: Use a paintbrush to anoint the birthday candle with the essential oil, brushing in upward strokes.

Step 2: Use the lighter to melt the bottom of the candle, then place it in the middle of your agate slice, upright.

Step 3: Place your rose quartz close to your candle to promote and enforce your intention of self-love

Step 4: Light the candle. Sprinkle the Himalayan pink salt in a circle around the candle to offer an extra layer of protection.

Step 5: Meditate in front of your burning candle. Think about everything about yourself that you love. Feel that self-love with every fiber of your being. If you find yourself thinking about a negative situation that happened, try to turn it into a positive one. For example, if you start to think about something you said to a coworker that you felt was embarrassing, try to flip it around by thinking: "Yes, that was embarrassing, but everyone does embarrassing things sometimes, and that is what makes us human. These feelings are normal, and I still love myself. Accidentally saying something embarrassing does not make me any less loved or important."

Step 6: Allow the candle to burn out completely as you meditate in silence. This takes anywhere from ten to fifteen minutes. Allow positive feelings to engulf you.

Invitation of Love Spell

This spell will help to attract love into your life and to let the universe know that you are ready to love and to be loved.

Ingredients:

- Three white candles

- Rosemary (a small piece is fine)

- One rose quartz crystal

- Incense (vanilla preferably)

- One small, red box (a gift box is perfect)

- Pink or red felt-tip or pen

- Patchouli essential oil

- Three candle holders

- An item that you personally feel represents love

Step 1: Find a place, either outdoors or indoors, that you feel safe and relaxed. Make sure it is relatively quiet, so you do not get distracted. A garden, forest, or even a favorite room in your place of living is perfect.

Step 2. Spend some time meditating to clear your mind of any distracting thoughts. When you feel ready, anoint all three candles with the patchouli oil.

Step 3: Place the candles in the candle holders and the holders directly on the floor or ground. It does not matter what position you put them in. Begin to chant:

"Love is in my life and has come to me.

I am in love, and they are in love with me."

Step 4: Place the rose quartz in the box, along with the item that you chose earlier. You can even write out a list of qualities you look for in a lover and use the list as your item. The box, with the items inside, focuses your intent and represents what love means to you.

Step 5: Hold your box in your hands. Allow yourself to be overwhelmed by feelings of love as you imagine what you will feel when the happiness awaiting you is finally yours. Imagine yourself in love. Take the time to meditate on these thoughts.

Step 6: Think of some affirmations that have to do with your desires. For example, "I will be loved" works well. Light your candles and chant the affirmation you chose repeatedly.

Step 7: Purposely deliver your intentions into the universe by saying, "so mote it be." Snuff your candles out, then close the box shut. Do not open it until the love you asked for arrives into your life. After your desires are fulfilled, then you may remove the crystal and keep it nearby as a reminder of what the universe provided.

Fire Flowers Spell

This spell is intended for those who have severed ties with a lover, or even just a relationship with anyone that caused distress and feel as if they are isolated from any sort of love in their life. It also works for those who are looking to uncloudy a pathway to a brand-new relationship.

Ingredients:

- Pencil and Paper

- A cauldron or any container that is fireproof

- One pink candle

- A candle holder or a safe dish

- Three dried white flowers (for example daisies, lilies, daffodils)

- The essential oil of your choice

- Incense (rose preferably)

Step 1: Choose a quiet, undisturbed place to cast this spell. Use a lighter or a match to light the incense, and let the smoke cloud the area.

Step 2: Place the candle in its holder or on a safe dish and light the candle.

Step 3: Gently remove the petals from one of your chosen flowers, one at a time. As you do this, chant the following words:

"I am (inhale at this time)

Full of power (exhale)

A powerful love (inhale)

That burns like fire (exhale)"

Step 4: Begin to remove the petals from the other two flowers, and say the incantation again once for each flower. When you are done, place the petals in your cauldron or the incense burner.

Step 5: Take a slow, deep breath. Clear your mind of distracting thoughts. When you are focused, use the pencil to write your full name on the piece of paper.

Step 6: Use the candle's flame to light a corner of the paper on fire. Place the paper in the burner or cauldron so that it can burn undisturbed.

Step 7: Allow the paper and the candle to burn completely. When the paper turns to ashes, and the candle wick is burned out, bury the flower petals and ashes, preferably in a flowerpot or a garden. Do the same with the candle, but keep it separated from the other items. Say thanks to the universe and the deities.

Wealth Attraction Bath

This bath cocktail can be used at any time, but it's most effective if you use it just before something important that could bring money your way. For example, just ahead of a business meeting, job promotion or financial opportunity. You need:

- A couple of tablespoons of sea salt

- 3 drops of basil oil

- 3 drops of cinnamon oil

- 3 drops of pine oil

- A small amount of dried patchouli

- A small bottle, such as a travelling bottle for toiletries

Run your bath and add the oil and herbs. Soak for at least 15 minutes, and visualize the outcomes you want from the meeting or event, and how you want it to bring wealth to you. Before you drain the bathwater, fill the bottle and take it with you.

Law of Abundance Spell

This spell needs to be cast on the night of a full moon. Take a check from your check book and leave the date line empty. On the payee line, write your full name. In the amount box, write 'Paid in Full,' and on the line where the words should be written, write the same thing. On the signature line, write 'Law of Abundance.' Place the check somewhere safe and special to you. You are not actually asking for something, just for anything that may be due to you, which is why it works – 'need not greed.'

Lavender Money Spell

For this spell, you need a conjure bag, which is a red flannel bag used for magickal purposes. If you want to make one, you can find directions online, or you can get a witch to make one for you. The magick will probably be stronger if you make your own though.

Once you have your conjure bag, you need seven money items of different denominations, depending on your home currency. Your money will increase by seven times, or even seven times seven.

Mint Prosperity Spell

This spell needs to be cast in a sacred circle, in which you'll need to have a mint plant and your wallet. Once the circle is cast and the quarters called, take the mint to the Earth Quarter and draw a pentagram over it with your hand. Return the mint to the altar and rub it over your wallet. Now place a mint leaf in the wallet and carry it with you to attract prosperity.

All of these spells will work for you if you need wealth. It's perfectly natural to wish for wealth, and if you practice witchcraft, the next progression is to think you can cast a spell for wealth. However, do you need that wealth, or is greed telling you that you need it? If you are just wanting to build your bank balance, and don't really need more money, the wealth spells just won't work for you. You really need to understand that, and also understand that wealth isn't always measured by money.

Chapter 7: The basic and advance practice of candle magic

Candle magic is perhaps the least difficult type of spell casting, and all things considered, it doesn't require a ton of extravagant ritual or complex apparatuses. As it were, anybody with a light can do magic.

Recollect when you made a desire before you extinguished the candles on your birthday cake. A similar thought applies to flame enchantment, just rather than simply seeking after your desire to work out as expected, you're announcing your expectation. Things being what they are, the birthday candle ritual depends on three key supernatural standards:

- Decide on a goal.

- Visualize the end result.

- Focus your intent, or will, to manifest that result.

Types of Candles

Candles come in all shapes and sizes. You will find a wide variety among different occultist shops, body shops, or even grocery stores. It helps, however, to buy from shops that specialize in magickal intent so that if you have any questions, there will be somebody there who likely knows what they are talking about, compared to an average grocery store clerk.

The majority of witches and those who practice magick rituals will tell you that the size of the candle is not important, but if the candle is too big and takes three days to burn out, you may not want to use those in a spell that requires the candle to burn all the way down naturally, which is a requirement in most spells. Therefore, a giant, bulky candle can actually be counterproductive.

The main types of candles are tea lights, votive, tapers, columns, encased pillars, and free-standing pillars. All of these types can be used interchangeably, but the best kinds of candles to use in spells that require them to be burned all the way are votive and tapers. This is because their wicks are typically short, and they are generally the easiest to control. One of the most popular candle types are the menorah candles, which are about four inches in length and are sold in bulk at easily accessed places, such as the grocery store. They are white, thin, and unscented, which make them perfect for most kinds of spell work.

In a few cases, a spell or ritual may need a specific kind of candle, such as a candle shaped like a certain figure to represent a specific person or a seven-day candle. Below is a short list containing the intent of a few commonly used candles in these cases.

- *Female figure:* This is used to attract or repel someone specific but can also be used to represent someone close to you who identifies as female.

- *Male figure:* This is used to attract or repel someone specific but can also be used to represent someone close to you who identifies as male.

- *Couple:* Candles shaped like a couple are used to bring a married couple closer together.

- *Genitalia:* This one is pretty straight forward. It is used for arousal, passion, sexual desire, and fertility.

- *Buddha:* Good fortune, abundance, and luck

- *Devil:* A devil-shaped candle is used for temptations, whether to encourage or banish them.

- *The Cat:* This is used specifically for money spells, luck, or even protection.

- *Skull:* This candle shape is used to repel unwanted feelings or thoughts. It is also used for healing spells or cleansing.

- *Knob Candle:* The seven knobs that make up the body of this candle represent seven wishes.

It is highly suggested that you use a candle that has never been used for spell work. Don't just pick up a candle that you burned for your nighttime bath and use it in a money spell because you do not have anything else. If you do not feel like going out and buying a new candle that day, you should save your spell work for another day. According to most magickal beliefs, a candle, once lit, absorbs the vibrations caused by the many items around it. It is believed that this may lead to a negative or ineffective magickal outcome, so you must exercise caution.

Colors and What They Mean to a Wiccan

In our world, colors have many purposes. They are used in art to express a certain intention or mood, to stimulate the mind with subtle or winding patterns, or even to organize. To a Wiccan, colors play a vital role in spell casting and intent. Each color has a role and intention for our everyday lives. Certain days, feelings, and even numbers have a connection to a certain color.

Candles, with their superb symbolic qualities, allow us to work directly with the magickal properties that they possess. For hundreds of years, humans have associated different colors with certain qualities or events. For example, passion and love have always been associated with the color red, as it is the color of blood and the heart. The color green is ever-present during the growing season of the earth and, therefore, has long been associated with abundance and prosperity.

In order to accurately cast the spells highlighted in this book, you will need to choose your candle's color carefully, and, ideally, perform the spells on the day of the week in which the intent is clear. Utilizing these color and time correspondences in your magick reinforces the intent of your spell and makes it more potent.

Red: Red is a symbol of vitality, passion, intense emotions, fertility, desire, sexuality, and strength.

White: White represents purity, healing, the beginning of a phase, the ridding of malicious spirits, peace, and innocence.

Pink: Pink is the color of love, friendship, affection, reconciliation, and harmony.

Purple: Purple represents spirituality, wisdom, idealism, devotion, and spiritual strength, insight, and emotion.

Black: This color rids negativity. It represents protection, stability, dignity, and the end (but also seed to a new beginning).

Blue: Blue symbolizes healing, truth, wisdom, protection, spirit, and patience.

Brown: Brown represents solidarity, grounding, strength, endurance, and unity with nature.

Yellow: This color symbolizes happiness, achievement, inspiration, knowledge, completeness, and imagination.

Green: The color green represents abundance, wealth, growth, prosperity, employment, balance, and renewal.

Gold: Gold represents integrity, inner strength, self-realization, intuition, and understanding.

Silver: Silver is the color of intuition, vision, purity, healing, capacity, memory, and intelligence.

Orange: This color represents energy, stimulation, vitality, communication, happiness, and attraction.

Grey: Grey symbolizes contemplation, stability, reserve, and neutrality.

Monday: Monday is ruled by the moon, and deals with fertility, insight, wisdom, beauty, illusion, emotions, and dreams. The colors best used on this day are blue, white, and silver.

Tuesday: Tuesday is ruled by Mars, and deals with victory, success, courage, defense, logic, vitality, conviction. It is a good day to cast problem-solving spells. The colors best used on this day are black, red, and orange.

Wednesday: Wednesday is ruled by Mercury, and deals with luck, change, fortune, creativity, education, insight, and self-improvement. The colors best used on this day are orange, purple, and grey.

Thursday: Thursday is ruled by Jupiter, and deals with prosperity, wealth, healing, abundance, and protection. The best colors to use on this day are purple, green, and blue.

Friday: Friday is ruled by Venus, and deals with love, fertility, birth, romance, passion, friendship, and pregnancy. The best colors to use on this day are green, pink, and blue.

Saturday: Saturday is ruled by Saturn, and deals with wisdom, change, cleansing, motivation, and spirituality. The best colors to use on this day are black, purple, and brown.

Sunday: Sunday is ruled by the Sun, and deals with promotion, success, fame, prosperity, and wealth. It is a good day to cast money spells. The best colors to use this day are gold, yellow, green, and orange.

Now that the days and the colors have been covered, it is time to choose a candle. To choose the color, it is best to correlate your intentions with the color you pick and the day that you cast the spell. For example, if you want to cast a spell that will multiply your wealth, you will want to use gold, yellow, or green candle and cast a spell on a Sunday.

 The potency of your desired spell entirely depends on how you choose to organize it. The closer you cast the spell to the intended day and with the right color, the more potent it will be. This is why it is of dire importance to choose your candle with deep thought and preparation.

Candle Magic Spell for Drawing Money

This spell is an easy and fun way to manifest more money in your life. It will bring together some of the other magical items you have learned about and will involve the use of a few additional items as well.

You will need the following:

- 3 green spell candles + holders

- Matches or a lighter

- Vervain essential oil

- Dried mint, crumbled into small pieces

- Dried basil, crumbled into small pieces

- A piece of parchment paper

- A carving tool, to carve a symbol into the wax (a pin, a needle, or knife)

- Several coins of various shapes, sizes, and country of origin

Steps for the Candle Magic Spell for Drawing Money

1. Cast a circle as desired.

2. At the altar, set your 3 green candles in an arc or semi-circle so that the top of the arc is away from you on the altar.

3. One at a time, pick up a candle and perform the following:

- Carve any symbols of prosperity that you like or that are a part of your practice into the wax, anywhere on the candle and all over the candle (you can look at runes and Celtic symbols if you aren't sure where to start). Rub off any wax that naturally sheds from carving.

- Rub essential oil on the candle (you can use your own blend and have it diluted in a carrier oil if that is desired).

- On the parchment paper, sprinkle the dried herbs so that they are all mixed together.

- Roll the anointed candle on the herbs and collect them on the outside of the candle.

- Say the following words or something similar, as you go through these steps for each candle:

"Candle magic born with me,

Help me to manifest my destiny.

I ask for money, riches, and wealth,

To come to me in the right good health.

This candle green will burn my truth,

To call to me abundance, forsooth.

The powers that be will hear my call,

To become richer now, and that is all.

And so it is"

4. With each candle carved and anointed, they can all be in their holders in the semi-circle as you sprinkle the coins in front of them, saying the following words:

"Money brought, and money sent,

I ask for riches by divine rite lent.

With open arms, I ask of thee,

To send me money, three times three!

So mote it be!"

5. Light the candles, and let them burn all the way to the end of the wick until they each go out.

6. If you have any remaining herbs from your candle rolling, you can now use them to light as incense on top of a charcoal disk in your cauldron.

7. Close the circle and bury the coins in the ground of your yard or garden.

This money spell can be modified to your own liking, but you can get a better picture of a fun way to use candles in your rituals and spells, using some other magical items and supplies.

Candle Magic Spell to Celebrate Imbolc

Imbolc is a time of year to celebrate the dawn of the Maiden (Triple Goddess) and the coming of Spring. It is a ritual typically celebrated with a lot of candles and the color white. You can modify this spell to your liking.

You will need the following:

- 10 white spell candles + holders

- Jasmine essential oil + carrier oil if desired (or Spring blend of your liking)

- White flowers of any kind

- Matches or lighter

- Hyacinth incense or a fragrance of first spring flowers

Steps for Candle Magic Spell to Celebrate Imbolc:

1. Cast your circle as desired.

2. Anoint each of your white candles with essential oil while you ponder the magic of the Maiden Goddess. You can even speak to her directly as you consecrate your candles.

3. Set them in their holders, and place them all over your altar space. You can also place them in other areas around the altar, as long as they are in places where they are seen and safe.

4. Light your incense of choice and lay the white flowers around. Try to place a few flowers near or next to each of your candles so that each one has a flower spray near it.

5. If you have flowers left over, you can set them anywhere that feels right. You can also just use flower petals if it is easier or more affordable than whole bunches of flowers.

6. Begin to light the candles and speak the following words, or something similar, as you do:

"Oh, Maiden Goddess of beauty bright,

Welcome back from Winter's night.

I ask you now to join me here,

By candlelight and flowers dear.

I welcome thee with all my heart and soul,

To bridge the gap between the dark and light worlds.

The time has come for Spring to be sprung,

Welcome, oh Maiden, may your powers be done!

And so it is."

7. Enjoy some delicious foods, herbal teas, or other brews as you sit by the candlelight and welcome the dawn of Spring with the Maiden divine.

Any spell can be enhanced with a little candle magic. Fire brightens your cause and purpose and joins every element together into one instrument of magic. Continue working with all the different colors, crafts, and variations of how to make magic with candles, and let them deliver your message to the Great Divine.

Most candle spells require the candle's flame to burn all the way down naturally, on its own, without being disturbed. However, it is hardly a good idea to leave a flame unattended, even in the form of a candle. Staying with the candle as it burns down could take hours, depending on the kind of candle one uses, and most do not have the time to spare. If you absolutely must leave your candle, simply place it in a safe place away from any flammable objects. An empty tub or sink are examples of safe places to leave the candle while you go about your daily business. It is also important to note that many oils used for anointing can be highly flammable and must be used with care. Some spells require the candles to be snuffed out, and it is easy for one to forget that there is oil on their fingers as they try to pinch the candle out. Handle these oils with extra caution.

As you explore and practice the magickal qualities of candles, you will soon take note that if you exercise the appropriate cautions and keep your focus, as well as a sincere intent, with harm to none, of course, you will begin to see your spell work flourish with success.

Chapter 8: Casting Circles

Casting circles is one of the basic skills used in witchcraft. It often the first thing that beginners will learn. The idea of casting circles is a bit complex, even if the techniques tend to be simple.

Casting a circle or circle-casting is the practice of creating a temporary space to perform a ritual or magic. By definition, it is round. While circle-casting is most commonly used by Wiccans, other Witches from different religions cast circles as well. The circle is a temporary temple, an area away from the ordinary world that can hold the magic you are working.

Typically, a circle is cast at the beginning of a rite by the high priestess and/or priest. Solitary practitioners are able to cast circles as well. After the spell work is done and the ritual is completed, the circle is released.

The circle is not a physical, but psychic boundary. It is not felt or seen by your regular senses. However, a circle can be detected energetically. It is also believed that this circle extends throughout all worlds and not just within our physical plane.

Why Should I Cast a Circle?

There are many different things that can interfere with your magic. Chaotic entities that feed your power, people with contrary wills, distractions from the world, are a few things that can interfere. Having a circle casting is one way to help shut out these influences and keep yourself focused. A magical trance can be psychically vulnerable, so a lot of witches will cast a circle to help protect their minds.

The outer barrier isn't the only important barrier of the circle. The inner barrier is just as important. Magical energy often bounces around and scatters throughout the Universe. The point of performing magic and rituals is to concentrate your energy on a purpose. Having a circle will allow you to gather more energy and hold onto it. If you call upon certain deities or spirits, a circle will offer them a cozy place to be during your rite.

So, you could say that a circle is meant to keep disturbances out and energy in. While this is very much a simplification, it is an easy way to look at it. It can also be viewed as a tool to improve the strength of your magic.

Do I Have to Cast a Circle?

You do not have to cast a circle. Not every tradition uses a circle. Egyptian, Norse, and other folk and shamanic magic practitioners work will without one. It is simply a useful technology and not a hard-and-fast rule.

How Big and What Shape Should My Circle Be?

The traditional size for a Wiccan circle is nine feet in diameter. Nine, or three times three, is a very important thing in Wicca. In many traditions, and within most covens, they will have a ritual nine-foot cord. They fold it in half and anchor it in the center and walk around in a circle to trace the circle's edge

Now, that's not to say you have to have a nine-foot circle. This is simply a suggestion. You can tailor your circle to the space you have available. You can make it too small, though.

To figure out if it is too small, gather your spell tools and yourself in the space you were thinking about using. If the circle you cast is so small that you could accidentally penetrate its edges while gesturing or reaching for something, then it is too small. Now, if the circle is being cast for a coven, the circle should be big enough so that everybody can maintain a comfortable distance from one another.

If, like most solitary practitioners, you only have a bedroom or study of some sort to work your magic in, a nine-foot circle is definitely not practical. It is better to have a smaller circle than a large circle that extends through furniture and walls. You typically don't want anything more in your circle than you, your altar, and tools for your spell work.

Casting Your Circle

It is always good to check and double check to make sure that you have everything with you before you cast your circle. Have your altar set up, your book of shadows with you, all of your spell and ritual tools, and anything else you may need in your space before you start casting your circle. Most people do not want to walk through their circle to get something once it has been cast. That said, if an emergency arises and you do need to leave quickly, then do so. Nothing catastrophic is going to happen if you leave your circle before closing your circle. A child and pet can also walk through your circle, and it won't disrupt anything.

Also, some people will draw a "door" if they need to leave their circle before their spellwork is finished using a wand or athame. You can also pretend that there is a "curtain" there that you walk through. When you reenter your circle, simply walk around the edge in a clockwise circle to help strengthen it again.

One last note before we jump into the circle casting methods, there are two words that you need to learn that may show up in some spells. The first is deosil. Deosil means clockwise. The second is widdershins. Widdershins means counterclockwise.

Simple Circle Cast

To begin, you will need to mark your circle. You first need to figure out where you want your circle to be. It doesn't matter if you are using the space where your altar is, doing it outside, or in your bedroom, you want to make sure it is somewhere you aren't going to be disturbed.

While you don't have to, some people will physically mark their circles with something meaningful. You can use a cord, crystals, or candles to mark your circle. You can also use crystals that correspond with the cardinal point.

Next, you will need to conjure up some energy that is going to protect and surround you and your work. Place yourself in the middle of what will be your circle. Allow yourself to relax and take a few deep breaths. Imagine that the top of your head is starting to open up like a funnel to take in a divine, white light. This is the crown of your head is will always have a strong connection with the Divine. You can open this up and amplify it whenever you want.

Bring your arms out so that your palms are facing out. Every time you take a breath in, picture yourself pulling all of that light into your crown, and every time you breathe out, push the light out through your palms to surround you with a protective shield. As your space fills with all of this energy, you may notice that you start to buzz or tingle, develop goosebumps, or feel uplifted.

Using the arm you write with, stretch it out to the side and point to the edge of your circle. Spin, three times, in a clockwise direction as you mentally mark your circle using this divine light. Bring both hands above your head and say: "I ask that the God and Goddess bless this circle so that I might be free and protected within this space. So mote it be."

Your circle is now cast; you can start to perform your ritual or cast spells. To close this circle, simply spin counterclockwise and feel the protective light dissipate.

Advanced Circle Casting

You'll need a compass and four candles. The four candles can be all white, or you can have one blue, one red, one yellow, and one green.

To start, take your compass and find the four cardinal points. Put the candles at each of these points. If you have the colored candles, the green one goes at North, yellow at East, red at South, and blue and West.

Begin at the North candle, light it, and repeat: "Guardians of the North, element of Earth, I call upon thee to be present during this ritual. Please join me now and bless this circle."

Move to the East candle, light it, and repeat: "Guardians of the East, element of Air, I call upon thee to be present during this ritual. Please join me now and bless this circle."

Move to the South candle, light it, and repeat: "Guardians of the South, element of Fire, I call upon thee to be present during this ritual. Please join me now and bless this circle."

Move to the West candle, light it, and repeat: "Guardians of the West, element of Water, I call upon thee to be present during this ritual. Please join me now and bless this circle."

Take your wand or athame and point it towards the edge of your circle. Walk in a clockwise direction three times and picture a white light rushing into the crown of your and being pushed out through your arm and through your tool, to the edge of your circle.

Take your place in the middle of the circle and feel your circle being filled with divine light. Say: "God and Goddess, guardian angels, and spiritual guides, please be present with me during this ritual. Bless this circle and keep me protected. No unwanted entities are welcome here; only pure, divine beings are invited into this space. This circle is cast. So mote it be."

You can now start your ritual and spellwork. When closing the circle, make sure you blow out your candles in the opposite order you lit them and thank the elements for being present.

Circle Casting

This is a rather simple circle casting, but you are going to need three, four, six, or nine things of a certain object. You can pick whichever number and whichever item resonates with you, but each other should be objects that are similar. For example, you could use four houseplants, nine candles, three rocks, or six seashells. If you have any sacred items, feel free to use those.

To cast your circle, start by holding your objects in your hands and create the intention for them as you move around your circle and place them to mark off the edge of your circle. If you are using candles, you will want to make sure that you have them placed on something safe so that you can light them safely without them catching something on Fire.

If you feel there are some words you would like to say as you do this, you can do it now, but this circle casting does not require that. Once you have placed all of your items, you are free to do your spell or ritual work.

To close this circle, all you need to do is pick your items in the opposite direction that you placed them.

Closing Your Circle
Once all of the work has been done, you will need to close your circle. When you release your circle, it gives the energies within a chance to dissipate and the room to return to its pre-ritual state. There are many different ways to close your circle, like ringing a bell, performing the casting in reverse, or picturing the walls dissolving. Gathering up your tools and putting them away will also help to scatter out the energy.

If you forget to close your circle, or you simply don't close it well, the circle will eventually fade on its own in a few minutes or hours. If you regularly use that area for your ritual work, then it may slow down the dissipation. That doesn't mean you should make it a habit to just walk away. You should always close your circle.

Chapter 9: Meditation and Dreams

It is scientifically proven that meditation is good for everyone. It connects you to your mind, body, and spirit on all levels and helps you attain a higher state of awareness while it promotes physical health. Meditation is often linked to spirituality and its many practices and you may not think it would be involved in the Wiccan practice, but it is one of the main attributes.

In almost every spell and ritual I perform, there is a moment of meditation. I have to meditate in order to connect with my inner knowing and the divine source energy I am working with. It only takes a few moments and it brings me into deeper closeness with the energy of all things, providing me with the ultimate balance.

Meditation isn't something you have to teach yourself how to do well; it comes naturally during your craftwork and if you are simply open to being with yourself and your Magick, then you are in meditation. Overall, meditation is just a natural part of communing with your own soul as well as the soulful energy present in all things in life.

The purpose of learning to be a witch is to enhance your life. You can do this with magic. You can find yourself entirely engulfed in a new and more adventurous lifestyle. Enhancing your life with magic takes a lot of practice.

Magic is not something that comes easily to most people. It takes getting out of your head to achieve anything. Life enhancement is a big part of the Wiccan culture, and that is what draws a lot of people to it.

However, despite a lot of people being drawn to this religion, there are a lot of people that leave it as well, and that is because they are not willing to put in the effort when it comes to enhancing their lives. They expect just to say a few phrases and the magic happens. This is due in part to how the media portrays magic. Look at the popular television series Charmed. It shows three witches who fight evil, and all they do is use a few simple spells, and that is not reality. The same goes for most literature out there. Wiccans are portrayed as people who get together in the woods, say a few spells, wave a few herb sticks, and boom—magic. It is harder than these portrayals.

Spells take practice and require executing multiple times to master results. There are also several different parts to spells that you must master, once mastered; you get to move on to the next level and practice those spells for hours on end before you get any results. To become a powerful witch, you must put in a lot of time and be dedicated to your craft. The cost of being lazy will have you remain at the same level for ages.

You cannot expect life enhancement to make your life one of leisure. This is yet another reason people leave Wicca. They expect to be able to make their crush fall in love with them and to use magic to become rich, and that just doesn't happen—at least not right away. Those things take hard work and dedication.

People have also joined and fell off the wagon, by becoming black witches. They found out ways to make themselves rich, and force someone to fall in love with them. However, that magic comes at a price, and the price is not cheap.

These people will literally sell their souls to a demon to achieve what they want. You want to stay away from these witches. If one were to die from a black witch, their soul would be tortured for all eternity. You will not be reincarnated; you will be sent straight to purgatory.

Purgatory is where the spirits of people who have done evil things and used black magic go to in the afterlife. It is not where you want to end up. Your spirit will be torn to pieces every day until the end of time, and even though your body will be dead, you will still be alive to feel it because you are your spirit. Let those who join Wicca and turn to black witches' parish on their own accord.

Anyways, how do you enhance your life with magic? You connect with the earth. You connect with other people. You fill your life with things that will enrich you and bring you joy. These things are possible with magic. It may seem that magic can't do anything that you can't do yourself, and maybe there may be some truth to that. However, being in the Wiccan religion, it makes it a lot easier to do these things with magic, rather than without magic.

Here's how magic can help you enhance your life:

Making Friends - Friends are hard to come by, and even if you have a big group of friends, they may not be the best of friends to have. As humans, we are attracted to what is known as shiny people.

These are usually the people that are fun to hang out with. However, these shiny people are generally not the best people to be around, as they seem only to hang around if you can do something for them. Humans are also easily drawn in by dramatic people. These people are the ones that are always loud, and always doing something that they shouldn't be doing. It is exciting, and it is fun. However, if they turn on you, it can be an unpleasant experience. These people can be toxic, and toxicity is the best way to ruin a friendship.

You want to hang onto these people because you think that they bring a lot of joy to your life, but the truth is they are only dragging you down. Usually, people feel obligated at the requests of shiny people—starting to ring any bells? To spot a toxic friend all you should do is try to do something that you want to do for yourself or ask for a favor, and watch them try to drag you down or not participate.

This is where magic comes in. Magic will draw in the right type of friends so that you can make a lasting bond with them, and not have to worry about them walking out of your life because you reach a milestone in your life, and can't take them to the mall twenty times a week anymore. Instead, these friends will root for you, encourage you to be the best that you can be, and they will not bat an eye when you do something to improve your life.

Magic will help you find the love of your life and someone who will bring you soup when you are sick. You will attract the type of person who doesn't care if you are wearing your pajamas all day or wearing a $300 dress when you see them. These friends are hard to come by, and magic will fill your life with these friends. This way you can ensure that you are making friends with the right kind of people.

Help You Find True Love - True love is the hardest to find. You may fall in love several times in your life, and you may even get married, but chances are it is not everlasting love. Love is everywhere, and at times it can be easy to find.

However, true love hard to find, because they are not looking for the right identifiers. They want excitement and butterflies forever, and while those are all well and good to have with your partner twenty years from now, the butterflies eventually fade, or they will not happen as frequently. When that happens, you want to be still able to wake up and kiss the person beside you good morning and feel good about it. If you don't, how will you ever love them for the rest of your life?

Find someone who even when the butterflies fade, gives you a warm feeling in your heart, and makes you happy. True love is the love where you can argue all day, and then laugh and be happy for months on end. True love is waking up next to the one you love, and seeing them in their most vulnerable state, and loving them even more.

This love is the love that people strive for endlessly, and it is a love that not a lot of people find. Some are tricked into thinking they found it because the butterflies last longer than usual, then they get married, and five years later, they get a divorce. This is because they just found someone that they lusted after longer than usual.

Enter magic. Magic will bring you someone who can make your heart race, and make you feel calm at the same time. It will bring you the person who will hold your hair when you are sick, and rub your feet when they are sore. It will bring you, someone, who will help with the dishes for the rest of your life. Someone who gets up with you at two in the morning to bake cookies when you can't sleep.

You want someone who is encouraging the Wiccan religion so that you can be yourself around them. Once you let go and let fate show you who you should truly be with, these spells will help take your relationships, and make them strong, and at the same time help you form a bond with someone to create an unbreakable relationship.

Letting fate take over is the hardest part. You want to find someone who you like, but most people do not trust fate to make that choice because they already have someone in mind to be their forever love. They do not want to relinquish that control for fear of something going away.

Are you going to fall in love with someone who is truly the one for you, or are you going to spend the rest of your life fighting with the person you married, and using countless spells to try to fix your relationship? The choice is for you alone, but with a little patience, and a little time, you will find the person that you have truly been waiting for.

Courage - If you are a person who is not particularly courageous in any aspect of life, do not fret. You are not alone. The average person has at least one area in their life where they lack in the courage department. This can range from being talking to strangers or trying to make it up in the business ladder. There are many parts of life that require courage; it is impossible to be courageous enough for all of them on your own.

For instance, you may be able to go skydiving, but the thought of talking to that gorgeous person who has caught your eye completely terrifies you. And that is okay because you can't be courageous at everything. Or maybe you are great at talking to people, and doing public speaking, but you are terrified to ride an elevator.

There are different fears out there, and you cannot conquer your fears without courage. A lot of people overlook magic and how it can boost your courage levels up. Courage is important, and spells can make you a little stronger. As a witch, it is one of the most important things you can have because you are going to have to stand up to people.

Whether it be to save an old tree from a company that wants to tear it down, or stopping a black witch from ruining someone's life, lots of acts require courage.

Magic can help, and it can bring you so much more than a little bit of courage. Magic can make you feel like you can take on the world. You will feel like you can do anything, and that is what you want. Just remember that the effects are not permanent, and you may have to reapply the spell a couple of times.

Magic gives you the courage until you find it on your own, after a few times of realizing how great it feels to stand up to something that terrifies you, you will not need the spell anymore because you will be able to be courageous on you own.

Luck - Luck is hard to come by, and lots of people need it. You need luck when you are playing the lottery, and you need luck when you ask the love of your life to marry you, and that is something that not a lot of people think of either. Just like courage, luck is something that you need to get by in life. It is not always hard work that you should rely on because sometimes, hard work can only get you so far. Such as in a big law firm, where you and the partner's pet are vying for a promotion.

You may do the harder jobs, and work the hardest, but they have the advantage of you because they are a favorite. In this case, a little luck may help. Luck can ensure that they are paying attention to your hard work, rather than having a clear winner picked out before the race even begins.

You can use a few simple spells to make talismans and good luck charms, as well as just cover yourself in an aura of good luck with some spells; these spells are generally not difficult. However, the more luck you desire, the stronger the witch you would have to be, because, the stronger the witch, the more powerful the spell. You also have to "reapply" less when you are more powerful. Even more, a reason to practice, right? Everyone wants to be lucky, so make sure to work on becoming the best witch that you can be.

A real-life scenario would be a job interview. You want to use these spells without abandon, because the more luck you have, the better off you will be in an interview, and you will hopefully land the job with ease. Don't get too cocky, even though you may apply and interview, if you are not a good fit, you may not get the job no matter how much magic you use.

Recall there is a major difference between confidence and being cocky. Confidence is knowing you can do the job. Being cocky is thinking that without any training you can do it better than everyone else. Cocky thinks that you are a shoe-in for a job you have never had any experience with. Confidence is knowing that you are a strong and quick learner and will be good at the job without any training. You want to be confident, yet humble. Know that you are not the perfect person for the job, but also know that you are the best candidate.

Clarity of Mind - Have you ever had a question that is burning in your mind or a decision that you had to make that was really hard? Did it take you longer than you care to admit to achieve what you wanted with these scenarios?

That happens to everyone at some point in their life, and it is entirely normal. You want to have a clear mind, and it is harder to achieve than you would think. And, even if you clear your mind, a lot of times it is still hard to find a clear answer. You search and search, but there are pros and cons to everything.

This makes it hard to find yourself the time to do what you want to do when you want to do it because you are still agonizing over making the decision or trying to figure everything out—decisions can be messy.

If you are having trouble figuring out where to go in life, you can use a spell to help you figure things out. There are many spells that help you open your mind to make the right decision, and a lot of it has to do with Divination. Yes, prophesying helps you make the right choices because you will be able to get an idea of what will be the outcome of your choice. There are spells out there to clear your mind, and there are spells to get the answers that you desire.

These spells are the ones that you want to use to find your way in life and really make the right choices. Perhaps you are wondering if your spouse is cheating, and you do not know if you should pursue the matter. Do a spell and get the answers you are looking for. Don't feel guilty if they are not cheating. You are not going through their personal effects, rather doing your research before confronting them and that is what a rational person does.

Banishing Evil - Let's face it, a lot of times, we are surrounded by evil. This world is a demonic playground, no doubt about it. In these times, it becomes harder to find a pure environment, and a lot of times those who are good are under attack from the world.

Have you ever felt like the entire world was against you, and even though the evil people seem to be living good lives, you are miserable?

That is what a lot of people deal with when they try to lead decent lives because it seems that life does not want good in it and rewards evil. There are ways to keep yourself pure and keep your environment pure as well. Have a good place to do your magic. You want your mind to be pure and clean from attacks of other, evil witches as well.

There are several spells out there for purifying not only the area but your mind as well. One of the most common spell types for purification is known as smudging.

If you are regularly practicing, you should probably smudge your area before each spell, but if you are not practicing often, once a week or biweekly should suffice. Just make sure that you purify it before you do a spell. The purer you keep it, the more effect your spells will have on your life and evil forces will not be able to counteract your spells.

There are several other spells that you can use to make sure that you are keeping your mind and environment pure from the evil that lurks around.

Candles are essential to this (white candles especially). They give you pure energy in which to perform your spells. White candles act as a channel directly to the Goddess herself to help you keep other entities from answering your calls. Although most spells do not call for white candles, it is best to light one whenever you do a spell.

Healing - As you a Wicca beginner, you can relieve side effects and many other issues that dwell under and on top of the surface of one's skin. Mental illnesses are something that you can help with. While you cannot cure these diseases, you can help alleviate the symptoms of things such as depression and anxiety.

You can also help someone who has PTSD sleep better at night. Magic when used to help people, including yourself, is wonderful. It also does not take a lot of magical strength to help alleviate the symptoms of illnesses, unlike with pain and suffering from a major physical injury.

Prosperity - Have you ever been unemployed and found yourself searching high and low for any source of income just to keep the lights on? It isn't fun, and nowadays it is getting harder to find jobs that are enough to pay the bills and keep food on the table. That is the downside of the world we live in. Jobs are becoming electronic and outsourced. And unfortunately, unless you live in a commune, you must have money to survive.

There are a lot of spells to help you have the upper hand with prosperity. It is a good idea to find a plethora of them to douse yourself with luck and prosperity if you are ever in need of it. The same goes for healing spells.

Master the Art of Meditation

It is best understood that meditation is a silence through which you can listen to your higher self. With concentration and focusing attention on the higher level of consciousness that exists in each of us, meditation helps. A daily meditation session can clear the cluttering mind and maintain a clear communication channel.

An Introduction to Meditation

It is best to describe meditation as' listening.' It is the art of hearing the Higher Self or the Inner Self. Some describe it as hearing the gods, or the creative force. It could simply be said that the Higher Consciousness is listening, even. All these things can be meditation. Meditation leads to personal advancement when used properly. Meditation is the simplest of all spiritual advancement techniques and can be practiced in a group or even on its own.

Meditation is a practice that calms the conscious mind, the mind that deals with everyday activities and life as you know it, and allows you to channel your higher consciousness, also referred to as subconscious, the part of your mind that is responsible for involuntary bodily functions, reflex actions, and what you might call' Universal Memory.'

The Dynamics of Meditation

To fully understand the dynamics of meditation, first the make-up of the human consciousness needs to be realized, and it needs to be recognized that humans are both physical and spiritual beings. These two facets of human nature are tied together at the vital centres, which are referred to by their Sanskrit descriptions –

Chakras. During the act of meditation, psychic energy travels through these chakras. The *kundalini* force is a potent force known as the 'Serpent Power', and once the *kundalini* flows within you, your chakras begin opening up in succession.

Mastering Meditation

If you approach the art with the wrong technique, or even simply approach the art without any technique at all, you may fail in meditation. Concentrating on your' third eye,' the area one inch above your brow line and one inch inward of your forehead, is believed to concentrate energy in your highest chakra. In the Third Eye meditation technique, the direction in which you focus your eyes also plays an important role. Turning your eyes above the horizon has to do with the energy in your higher consciousness and your spiritual energy. Focusing your eyes straight out is about your conscious mind, while focusing down is about the subconscious mind.

It is best to select a position to meditate in when performing meditation. Meditation is known to be performed in the lotus position conventionally, but this position is not always comfortable, so it is better to be comfortable in another position of your own choice.

You are free to assume any position as long as your spine is straight– either sitting on the floor, on a chair, or lying on your back. The more comfortable you are, the more energy and mind you can concentrate on. When selecting an area to do your meditation, it is important that the chosen space is quiet and, of course, your cleaned and censored circle will be the best choice.

However, if for whatever reason you select another space, it's best to clean up the space and censor it like you did with your Circle. While facing a specific direction in meditation is not necessarily important, facing the east is sometimes suggested.

Your comfort, however, is the most important thing, and so if you have a better view in another direction, do not hesitate to face it! You are also free to select the time of the day you meditate, as is the position you choose and the direction you face and the space you choose. It is best, however, to stick to that particular time of day to meditate every day so that your meditation is consistent. Thus, choosing the most convenient time is best, one that will be quiet and peaceful but still achievable every day.

It needs to be done consistently to remain successful and to be successful in meditation. Some recommend meditation between fifteen and twenty minutes a day, twice a day. You might get by with a single fifteen-minute session per day at the bare minimum. Consistency is key again– so it's important to stick to the number of sessions as well as the times.

How to Do a Wiccan Meditation

Wicca is really a modern religion full of ancient traditions of witchcraft. The practices of drawing from the moon and invocation of the goddess are identical to mediation, but you might deepen the Wicca practice and promote peace with the divine through daily meditation to improve clarity and serenity.

Grant your mind a deep meditation status.

Relaxation instruments like candles, incense, and singing will assist you in a relaxing relaxation state. You can listen to a singing CD or sing the name of your favorite deity or goddess. Keep the lights low or disable them.

Choose a relaxation spot that resonates with you.

You'll also want to practice your counseling outside if you practice Celtic Wicca. Your love for nature's sights smells and sounds your meditation. Most Wiccans prefer to mediate on their altars, especially when the weather is not good. The key is to choose a place to meditate that will naturally make you feel relaxed. Make sure the room is silent and not disturbed as you mediate indoors.

Find a convenient spot.

If you sit down or lie down or walk, as long as you are comfortable and relaxed, it doesn't matter. Your goal is to be alert and receptive, so don't fall asleep so comfortable.

Decide which kind of mediation you are going to do.

Passive meditation is the way to allow images to arise in your mind and to focus on these images or symbols. You should consciously meditate on the image or symbol on which you want to focus, with open or closed eyes. If you allow a symbol to enter you or if you choose the symbol, send the image that you have selected. Subjects to be considered include: Magic / magic God / Goddess

Magic(ies) Number(s)Tree(s), Flower(s) or plants Gems (crystalline, amethyst, sapphire,

Close your eyes. Close your eyes. Concentrate for a few minutes on your intake.

Observe breathing for yourself. Bring your sensing to your feet if your breathing is slow and steady and shift your focus all the way up to your body. Remove any tension in your body that you feel. You can also pause and reflect on stress and wonder why there is pressure

Visualize positive energy that fills your life.

Respire in and picture your feet with white light to the top of your head. Exhale the white light and let it loose into your magic space.

If you practice passive meditation, allow thoughts to surface.

If you are fascinated by a thought or image, start focusing on it, then let it go and allow the next thought to surface. When you choose to do active meditation, close your eyes, and focus your attention on the symbol or picture you have selected. (If your thoughts begin to fall, return to the focus of your breathing and start over.) You can keep your eyes open and concentrate on your preferred symbol if you prefer. Give it your full and look at all facets of it.

Maintain a notebook and pen in the area.

Perhaps you want to pick up ideas or draw pictures during your meditation. Go to your meditative state once you have done that. End your session with thanks.

Conclusion

Wicca is a powerful way of life. It is an essential reality that can bring you so much inner harmony, peace, abundance, fertility, and prosperity on all levels of your life. You can give great thanks to the life that you have as we are all here to live and seek our truth with the Great Mother and the Father Sky, held by the universe as we explore our eternal destinies and practice knowing who we are from deep within the blanket of Magickal truth.

I am here to give you all of that faith in yourself and knowledge of the Wiccan path so that you can further your own Magick and self-discovery. I hope that you have found the information that you needed to inspire an even deeper existence within the craft you are creating in your life.

Let these ideas, teachings, guidelines, and tutorials help you gain the confidence you need to support a fully alive and awakened Wiccan practice of your own. You are your true power and to worship the divine in all things is the essence of wholeness within your life and yourself.

As you move forward on your journey, continue to teach yourself new concepts, histories, methodologies, and transformations to help you build your practice into the work of art it is destined to be. Let your intuition be your guide and give you all of the courage you need to fulfill your dreams of Magick.

Anything you do from here forward will be a gift to getting yourself on track with your own spells, rituals, altar space, Book of Shadows and daily practices. There is such abundance in this way of life and so many ways to enjoy it. You can be truly crafty and creative with your work and your inner world to bring more harmony into your life, the second main take away from this book.

The final takeaway is that Wicca brings you into divine connection with all of the energies of the universe. It shows you that we all have a significant part to play in the energy of all creation and that as you practice your rituals and spells, you are declaring that you are present and available to live your life through Magick and awareness of all that is around you.

Take these lessons to heart and do with them what you will. Harm none and remember the Rule of Three. Let the blessings of life unfold through the seasons along with the cycles of the Sun and Moon. Give thanks to the wind, the water, the heat of the fire, and the firm soil underfoot. Breathe Magick into your life every day and ask to know what you must in order to keep growing in your powerful path of Magick.

Astrology and Numerology Academy

CPSIA information can be obtained
at www.ICGtesting.com
Printed in the USA
BVHW081958190421
605297BV00003B/625